大为和海琳在中国

大为和海琳在中国

大为和海琳在中国

中级汉语教材

David And Helen In China

Part I

With Online Media

Phyllis Ni Zhang 张霓

with

Yuanyuan Meng 孟苑苑
Donald K. Chang 张光诚
Irene C. Liu 刘瑞年

Yale UNIVERSITY PRESS   New Haven and London

This book was originally accompanied by a CD. The audio files are now available online at yalebooks.com/davidandhelen.

This is an **FEP** book.

Yale University Press books may be purchased in quantity for educational, business, or promotional use. For information, please e-mail sales.press@yale.edu (U.S. office) or sales@yaleup.co.uk (U.K. office).

Printed in the United States.

The Library of Congress has cataloged the CD edition as follows:

DAVID AND HELEN IN CHINA: An Intermediate Chinese Course,
Part One and Part Two (bound separately; sold as a set only)
(simplified character edition)
Phyllis N. Zhang with Yuann-yuann Meng, Donald K. Chang and
Irene C. Liu.
1. Chinese language
2. Chinese language; post-basic, for foreign speakers, English
3. High School and College I. Title
1999

ISBN 978-0-887-10216-5 (CD edition)
ISBN 978-0-300-22660-7 (online media edition)

A catalogue record for this book is available from the British Library.
10 9 8 7 6 5 4 3 2 1

大为和海琳在中国

David And Helen In China

大为和海琳在中国

目录 (Contents)

词类缩语表

Abbreviations of Parts of Speech

A:	adverb (e.g.,他真聪明；我也去；你们一块儿说。)
Adj.:	adjective (e.g.,小孩子，好学生,or as Predicate, e.g., 我们都好，可是很忙。)
AV:	auxiliary verb (e.g.,她真会说话；我不喜欢唱歌。)
BF:	bound form (character not to be used by itself; e.g., 右手；南边)
CV:	co-verb (e.g., 我跟你们说中文；老师对我们很客气。)
EV:	equative verb (e.g.,那个人是我哥哥；你姓什么？)
IE:	idiomatic expression (e.g., "没关系！"；"不敢当"；"哪里，哪里！")
Interj:	interjection (e.g., 啊！你来了；哎呀，我忘了。)
M:	measure word (e.g., 五个星期；好几张纸；十多封信)
MA:	movable adverb (e.g., 我虽然会说，可是说得不太好。)
N:	noun (e.g.,桌子；父母；衣服；咖啡；意思)
Nu:	number (e.g., 六；八百；两千多；四十几个人)
P:	particle (e.g., 你好吗？他怎么还没来呢？这孩子好高呀！)
PH:	phrase (e.g., 一路平安；好久不见)
Pref:	prefix (word used as the beginning of a compound; e.g., 男人；公共汽车)
PW:	place word (e.g., 这里；那儿；地方；北京；美国)
QW:	question word (e.g., 什么？怎么？谁？为什么？哪个？)
RV:	resultative verb compound (e.g., 看见；睡着；找到；搬出去)
RVE:	resultative verb ending (e.g., 看懂；睡着；找到；拿上去)
SP:	specifier (e.g., 这个人；那本书；每个国家；头两年)
Suf:	suffix (used as word ending; e.g., 我们；月底；录音机)
TW:	time word (e.g., 今天；上午九点；下礼拜；一九九五年)
V:	verb (with or without object; e.g., 来；打；买；知道；玩儿；教)
VO:	verb-object compound (e.g., 吃饭；说话；写字；走路；做事)
VP:	verbal phrase (part of a sentence; usually without subject; e.g.,做三顿饭；在这里住)

Other Abbreviations used

colloq: colloqial; used often in conversation   lit: literary; used often in writing or refined speech

re:refering to   sb: somebody   sth.: something   syn.: synonym

春节

—在中国过年—

第十课

Situation	Structure	Culture
语言情景	语言结构	文化介绍

In Lesson Ten you'll join 大为 to celebrate China's most festive time of year: the (lunar) New Year--The Spring Festival (春节). The Spring Festival, one of China's half-dozen or so official holidays, is a great time in China and you'll take a look at how 大为 and company prepare for this fun event.

In terms of grammar you will focus on how the passive voice, so much a part of English expression, is formed in Chinese. You'll want to take a look back at Lesson 8, where one element of the passive usages was introduced.

And culturally, you'll learn about some of the traditional activities associated with the very festive Chinese New Year.

春节

--在中国过年--

春节快到了，到处[i]都打扫得干干净净，装饰得漂漂亮亮：家家都在做过年的准备。

春节就是阴历的新年，是中国最古老也是最热闹的节日。按照阴历的算法[ii]，这是一年的开始，又刚刚进入春天，所以把这个节日叫作春节。春节期间有很多传统的风俗习惯和庆祝活动，如贴年画和对联、放鞭炮、拜年等等。年画、对联和鞭炮的颜色都是以红色为主，因为对中国人来说，红色代表喜事。

从前这些风俗习惯都跟迷信有关。比方说，从前人们怕鬼，以为在门上贴一张门神画，鬼来的时候就会被门神打跑；鞭炮的声音大，一放鬼也就不敢来了。现在大多数人已经不信鬼神了，贴年画、对联和放鞭炮都是为了使节日更漂亮、更热闹。新年到来的那天夜里有很多人是不睡觉的，鞭炮声也响一夜。

i. 到处 (dàochù,everywhere) always precedes the verb or adjective.
Examples: 到处都打扫得干干净净；到处都很热闹；你别把书到处放.

ii. 法 (way, method) is often preceded by a monosyllabic verb forming very handy noun phrases, often with general/abstract meanings ('way of DOING A VERB'). Here are some examples: 算法 (calculation), 看法 (opinion, viewpoint, way of looking at things), 想法 (idea,thoughts), 用法 (usage, method of using), 说法 (interpretation, explanation, theory).

春节	春節	Chūnjié	N Chinese New Year ("Spring Festival")
过年	過年	guò//nián	VO to observe the New Year
装饰	裝飾	zhuāngshì	V/N to decorate; decoration
历	曆	lì	BF calendar (used as N-Suf.)
阴历	陰曆	yīnlì	N lunar calendar
阳历	陽曆	yánglì	N solar calendar
古老		gǔlǎo	ADJ ancient
节日	節日	jiérì	N holiday, festival
按照		ànzhào	CV according to
算法		suànfǎ	N calculation, way of calculating
入		rù	V [lit.] to enter (syn. of 进)
进入	進入	jìnrù	V to enter (syn. compound)
期间	期間	qījiān	TW during [a period of time]
传统	傳統	chuántǒng	N tradition
风俗	風俗	fēngsú	N custom, convention
庆祝	慶祝	qìngzhù	V/N to celebrate; celebration,
活动	活動	huódòng	N activities, events
如	如	rú	EV such as
对联	對聯	duìlián	N (poetic) couplets (two-line verses composed in parallel phrases/sentences)
放		fàng	V to release; set off
鞭炮		biānpào	N firecrackers
放鞭炮		fàng biānpào	VP to set off firecrackers
拜年		bài//nián	VO to pay New Year's tributes
迷信		míxìn	ADJ/N superstitious; superstition
鬼		guǐ	N ghosts
神		shén	N gods
被		bèi	CV (passive voice marker)
打		dǎ	V to hit, beat
跑		pǎo	V/RVE run, run away; (run) away
声音	聲音	shēngyin	N sound, voice, noise
大多数	大多數	dàduōshù	N/AV/A majority; most (people, etc.) mostly
响	響	xiǎng	V/ADJ (sth.) to make a sound; loud

春节的第一天，人们要穿上新衣服，向自己的亲友拜年。拜年就是大家互相问候、庆祝新年到来的意思。因为新年的到来是一件喜事，所以拜年的时候大家互相说“恭喜恭喜”或“恭喜发财”。小孩子给长辈拜年的时候，长辈按习惯要给小孩子一个“红包”。红包里面装的是钱，所以，小孩子们虽然不懂拜年是什么意思，可是都喜欢拿红包，当然也就高兴给长辈拜年了。

除了这些风俗习惯以外，在大街上和公园里还有很多表演，所以春节期间到处都很热闹。

春节的时候，大为和海琳一个在北京，一个在台北，可是他们很高兴能跟中国人一起过春节。大为要和几个同学一起到公园去看表演，他的中国朋友刘东还请他到家里去吃饺子。海琳的伯母春节的时候要在家里请客，准备了很多好吃的东西，其中还有海琳最喜欢的年糕。伯母想借请客这个机会给海琳介绍对象。海琳知道伯母的意思，她想，既然伯母要给她介绍那就让她介绍吧，完了以后就告诉伯母她不喜欢这个人就行了，那伯母还有什么办法？

问候	問候	wènhòu	V to ask after someone; to greet
到来	到來	dàolái	V/N to arrive; arrival
恭喜		gōngxǐ	IE "Congratulations!" (said on New Year's Day, birthdays, weddings, graduations, etc.)
发财	發財	fā//cái	VO to make a fortune; get rich
长辈	長輩	zhǎngbèi	N elders ("the senior generation"), seniors
红包	紅包	hóngbāo	N "red envelope" (used for giving money as a gift)
除了...以外		chúle...yǐwài	CONJ aside from, besides
表演		biǎoyǎn	V/N to give a performance; performance, show
刘东	劉東	Liú Dōng	N (name of a person)
饺子	餃子	jiǎozi	N (Chinese) dumpling
既然		jìrán	MA since (it is the case)
表演		biǎoyǎn	V/N to give a performance; performance, show

判断出以下词语的意思：

年画	年畫
喜事	
门神画	門神畫
打跑	
亲友	親友
请客	請客
年糕	

回答问题：

1. 中国的新年是怎么算的？为什么叫作春节？
2. 春节期间有些什么风俗习惯？这些风俗习惯是怎么来的？
3. 春节期间人们常吃什么东西？
4. 大为和海琳春节的时候有什么安排？

语言结构

Focusing on Structure

Using bèi (被)-Sentences for Passive Voice

The term passive voice in Mandarin is applied, generally, to sentences containing the word 被, which introduces the agent or doer of the action. In Chinese there are several ways to convey or imply passiveness. We will concentrate on one of the most common forms, the 被 sentence types.

Type I 被 sentences have the following word arrangement:

他被他爸爸打了。He was beaten BY his father.

被 marks the someone or something that was acted upon involuntarily by someone or something else (the agent). Notice how the verb occurs in the sentence-final position, just like the 把 construction.

Type II: An important variation is as follows:
他被骂了。 He was scolded.
Note here how the agent of the action is omitted.

她的帽子被（风）吹跑了。

窗子被（孩子）打坏了。

鸡肉被狗吃了。

The negative of a 被 sentence uses 没（有）in front of 被：
她的帽子没被（风）吹跑。

Note in the above examples that, generally, when the topic is human, 被 formulations are used

to express that something unfortunate has happened (or has not happened). However, in recent years, the use of 被 in messages that do not convey adversity has been increasing, probably due to the influence of Indo-European languages, especially English, on modern Chinese.
Example:

他被(大家)选作学生代表。 He was /has been elected (by everyone) as student representative.

For the language student it is essential to keep in mind that what is normally expressed in English by the passive is often not a 被 sentence in Mandarin.

Here are some examples:

他昨天说的话，大家都懂.	What he said yesterday was understood by everyone.
他受到很多人的喜爱。	He is/has been well-liked by many people.
那本书是他写的。	The book was written by him.

None of the above sentences is appropriate as a 被 sentence. The message of the first sentence is best handled by the Topic-Comment pattern of Mandarin, where the direct object of the verb serves as the Topic and then something is said about that Topic. In the second sentence, keep in mind that 受, another passive marker, is used for abstract verbs. And, in the third example, Mandarin uses the 是...的 construction to mark focus (here focusing on 他). In addition, the book does not exist when the action takes place, hence, not a 被 case.

So keep the following three conditions in mind when using 被:

1. The passive party (the initial element) does not have control over the other party (the agent of the action) introduced or implied by 被 or the action itself (usually imposed).
2. The passive party must already exist at the time of the action.
3. Except for future events, the action verb must have an extension or complement, such as an aspect marker, e.g. 了,过, a resultative complement, e. g. 吃完,拿走 ; or other extensions, e. g. 打了一下.

词汇用法

Word Usage

Verbs

- 装饰：装饰房间(商店...)；客厅装饰得很漂亮。/把房间稍微装饰一下。/我喜欢这种装饰(N)。/装饰品(Mod.)
- 庆祝：庆祝节日(新年、生日...)；好好庆祝庆祝；庆祝活动；开庆祝会(Mod.)
- 问候：问候长辈；向亲友问候；请代我向他问候。
- 进入：进入春天(公园、大学...)；还没进入大学以前
- 装：把钱装进信封里。/把信装在盒子里。/红包里面装的是什么？那个盒子太小，装不下这几本书。
- 响：电话响了两声；鞭炮声响了一夜；录音机开得太响(Adj.)

V-O Compounds; Resultative Verb Compounds/Phrases

- 请客：在家里请客；我上个月请了两次客。/明天的晚餐我请客。/他没钱请客。
- 发财：发大财；恭喜发财；他开了一个餐馆，发了一笔小财。
- 打跑：把鬼打跑；他被打跑了。/那只狗打不跑。
- 穿上：穿上衣服(鞋子...)；把鞋子穿上；衣服太小，穿不上。

Adjectives

- 古老：古老的节日(传统、风俗)；这个房子的装饰很古老。

Nouns

- 传统：中国的传统；古老的传统；传统节日(习惯、风俗、看法...)
- 风俗：风俗习惯；那个地方的风俗；传统的（古老的...)风俗
- 声（音）：说话的声音（说话声）；鞭炮的声音（鞭炮声）；听见一个奇怪的声音

Others

- 到处：房间里到处都是他的书。/你别把东西到处放。/他到处都有朋友。
- 期间：考试(春节)期间；一九八五年到一九九三年期间；我在美国(的)期间
- 大多数：大多数人都喜欢过节。/春节期间商店大多数都开门。

句型和习惯用语

Sentence Patterns and Expressions

1. A就是B的意思 (A means/refers to B)

- “亲友”就是亲戚和朋友的意思。“亲友” means “relatives and friends.”
- 她说她没时间来，其实就是她不想来的意思。
- “拜年”就是 ____________________
- Setting off firecrackers during the Spring Festival means to celebrate the arrival of the New Year.

2. .....以......为主 (...consists mainly of...)

- 年画的颜色以红色为主。
  The primary color used on Chinese New Year's posters is red.
- 今天的考试以听写为主。
- 这个学校的学生 ____________________
- Study is the main component of his daily life.

3. 按(照)...的V法，...... (According to ..., ...)

- 按照他的说法，电脑并不难学。
  According to his view, a computer is not hard to learn.
- 按照阴历的算法，这一天是一年的开始。
- 按照美国人的看法，____________________
- According to the manager's idea, we need to hire someone who is experienced in marketing. (推销 tuīxiāo)

4. .....按......V ([Sb.] does sth. according to...)

- 他从来不按规定做事。He never does things according to the rules.
- 我要你按我说的写。
- 你到了美国，就应该按美国人的习惯____________________________
- Do this as your teacher told you.

5. 除了......以外，也/还......(Besides..., sb./sth. also....)

- 除了他以外，我也（不）是中国人。Besides him, I'm also (not) Chinese.
- 除了这本书以外，我还有两本英文书。
  Besides this book, I have two other English books.
- In addition to her performance (acting), I also like the books she's written.

Compare:

除了他以外，我们都不是中国人。 None of us is Chinese except him.

我除了星期天以外，每天都去图书馆。 I go to the library every day but Sunday.

6. 把 A叫作 B (call A "B")

- 我们把这个节日叫作春节。We call this holiday the "Spring Festival.ã
- 在台湾，我们把 "Mandarin" 叫作“国语”。
- 因为小王长得很胖，所以他家里的人都____________________“小胖”。
- Some people call New York City “The Big Apple.”

7. A跟B有关 **(A [effect/result] has something to do with B [cause/source]...)**

- 这件事一定跟他有关。 This must have something to do with him.
- 从前很多风俗习惯都跟迷信有关。
- 他今天那么高兴一定跟____
- His return to China last week had to do with his mother's illness.

8. 既然……，那（么）**……(Since [that is the case], then....)**

- 既然她要给你介绍对象，那就让她介绍吧。
- 既然你不去，那我也就不想去了。
- 既然你不爱他，那为什么______________________________________?
- Since you have studied Chinese for five years, you must now be fluent in speaking.

文化介绍

Learning About Culture
春节期间的风俗习惯
Chinese New Year Customs

The Spring Festival, also known as the Chinese (Lunar) New Year, starts on the first day of the old lunar calendar. In solar calendar terms the festival usually falls during the last week in January or the first week of February. Although nowadays officially lasting only three days, the festival traditionally goes on for fifteen days. Many people take a week or more time off from work in order to properly celebrate the event. Marking the onset of spring and the beginning of a new year is an old custom that goes back more than two thousand years in China. Chinese people still consider the lunar New Year to be the most important holiday of the year. The holiday was first called yuándàn 元旦 "first morning" but later, when the solar calendar became official, 元旦 or xīnnián 新年 "New Year" became the standard term for the solar New Year's Day (i.e. January 1st), while the lunar New Year was usually called chūnjié 春节 "The Spring Festival." Most Chinese use this term nowadays.

春节 is a great occasion for feasting, shopping, visiting and all sorts of fun things. Because of the constant rounds of activity every family makes sure that great holiday food of all sorts are on hand for the family and visitors.

春节 is also a time for family reunions. Those who are away often feel the need to return home for this particular festival. It is an ideal situation for a reunion and a chance to commemorate family solidarity. The pace in most work units slows down to a crawl because staff often take time off to travel for sightseeing or visiting relatives and friends.

春节 concludes with yet another festival, the Lantern Festival (called 元宵节 yuánxiāo jié or灯节 dēng jié,), which falls on the fifteenth day of the first month of the lunar calendar. People take the opportunity to make or buy paper lanterns and the great variety of lanterns contributes to the colorful pageantry of this time of year. In the evening, the lanterns are placed and lighted on the main streets or hung in the crowded bazaars. The lanterns come in a fantastic number of shapes, such as fruits, flowers, animals and even human figures. The most popular lantern is called the "running horse lantern (走马灯)." It is constructed of revolving paper figures that, when lighted by a candle inside, throw shadows on a small screen. Hundreds and thousands of fun-loving adults and children flock around these lanterns, enjoying the spectacular show.

The Lantern Festival, like every other festival, has its own popular special food, yuánxiāo 元宵 (called tāngyuán 汤圆 in some parts of China). Yuánxiāo元宵 are snacks made of glutinous rice flour, round in shape and more than an inch in diameter with sweet ingredients inside. They are boiled until thoroughly soft.

With the excitement and fun of the Lantern Festival activities and the sweet taste of yuánxiāo, the Chinese people finally conclude their Lunar New Year celebration.

第十课听力练习

第一部分：单句

请你们听下面的句子。每个句子的意思是什么？请在三个选择中选出一句来。

1. (a)今天的庆祝活动不太热闹。
(b)今天的庆祝活动不包括放鞭炮。
(c)今天的庆祝活动主要是放鞭炮。

2. (a)公司怎么规定，我们就怎么做。
(b)我们不重视公司的规定。
(c)公司对我们没信心。

3. (a)那个德国人只会说英文和法文。
(b)那个德国人，英文、法文和中文都说得很流利。
(c)那个德国人会说的外语不包括中文。

4. (a)我们今天的晚饭以饺子为主。
(b)今天晚上我们没吃饺子。
(c)今天晚上我们又吃饺子又吃面。

5. (a)他对电脑没有兴趣。
(b)他只喜欢电脑，不喜欢别的。
(c)他是主修电脑的。

6. (a)他希望你被那家电脑公司雇用。
(b)他认为你很有希望被那家电脑公司雇用。
(c)他说那家电脑公司希望你赶快去上班。

7. (a)我不知道谁把我的红包拿走了。
(b)我不知道谁给了我一个红包。
(c)我忘了我把红包拿给谁了。

8. (a)房东想跟李先生买一套旧家具。
(b)李先生把那套旧家具卖给房东了。
(c)房东把那套旧家具卖给李先生了。

9. (a)“清”这个字没有什么意思。
(b)“清”就是水的意思。
(c)“清”的意思跟水有关系。

第二部分：短文

第一遍:请你们听懂这篇短文的大意，然后回答问题。

问题：这个人主要在谈些什么？

a)谈中国几个重要的传统节日　　b)谈她以前怎么过春节

第二遍:请你们读下面的句子，然后把这篇短文再听一次。听完后，看看这些句子说得对不对。

1.这个人最喜欢春节，因为她喜欢吃年糕。
2.这个人和她的家人在除夕(chúxī)当天才开始做过年的准备。
3.除夕是新年的第一天。
4.这个人在春节的第一天会早起向亲友拜年。
5.这个人今年没回家过年。

第三遍:请你们读下面的问题，然后把这篇短文一段一段地再听一次。听完每一段后，请回答问题。

第一段:　1.这个人最喜欢的传统节日是什么？
　　　　2.她为什么最喜欢春节？

第二段:　1.她的家人什么时候开始作过年的准备？
　　　　2.准备过年的时候，谁负责写对联？谁负责打扫房子？

第三段:　1.除夕(chúxī)是哪一天？
　　　　2.除夕这一天，她的家人还忙着作过年的准备吗？

第四段:　1.她在春节的第一天为什么会特别早起？
　　　　2.她以前怎么向住在远处的亲戚拜年？

第五段:　1.她今年在哪里过年？
　　　　2.今年的新年她为什么觉得很寂寞？

第十课 练习
词汇；句型；语法

I. 用适当的词填空：

1. 过：中国人每年过两次______。/我春节过______很快乐，你是怎么__________？

2. 庆祝：明天是你的生日，我们应该______________。/节日期间公园里有_______________。今年我们系里开了好几次____________，其中一次是庆祝_____________。

3. 传统：中国人过年有什么_____________？/传统的___________认为男人不应该做家务事。

4. 声/声音：鞭炮_______；她_______的声音太_______，我听不见。你能不能请她_________一点？/外面_______的声音太响，我睡不着。

5. 响：你别把收音机__________太响。/我听见电话铃响了_________，我刚去接，又不__________。

6. 期间：我（在）______________期间常到北京去。/____________学生们多半都回家了。

7. 到处：我进他的房间一看，WOW！______________________！/你别把东西________________。

8. 按照：按照___________________，过年的时候要吃饺子。/按照阴历的_________，新年不是一月一日。/你到了美国，就应该__________做事。/如果你按我说的______________，你一定学得很快。

9. 大多数：我的______________大多数是____________。/我们班大多数学生_______________。去年我大多数时间在_______________。

II. 把下面的句子改成"被"字句：

1. 他把我的车卖了。 ______________________

2. 我把那本书借给他了。 ______________________

3. 啤酒我们喝完了。 ______________________

4. 我的自行车他骑走了。 ______________________

5. 风把广告吹到地上去了。 ______________________

III. 把下面的句子改成否定句 (Change the following into negative sentences):

1. 他被人打过。 ______________________

2. 杯子被打破了。 ______________________

3. 鬼被打跑了。 ______________________

4. 我的病被他医好了。 ______________________

5. 我的书包被他拿走了。 ______________________

IV. 把下面的句子翻译成中文（哪个句子应该用"被"，哪个不应该？）

1. The book was written by an American in 1985.

2. The letter was finished yesterday.

3. The TV set was damaged by the child.（搞坏）

4. The books were moved to another room by my mother.

5. He was taught by that teacher.

V. 用"-法"改写下面句子中划线的部分：

1. 你能不能告诉我这个字怎么写？ ______________________

2. 我不同意你这样做。 ______________________

3.我不知道<u>这个字怎么用</u>。 ______________________

4.我想听听你<u>对这件事是怎么想的</u>。 ______________________

VI.<u>改写句子：</u>

1. 他的看法是，红色代表喜事。（按照......的V法，......)

2. 中国人把阴历新年叫作春节。（按照......的V法，......）

3. 你的老师怎么要求，你就怎么做。（按照......的.....Verb)

4. 他的工作主要是向国外推销新产品。（以......为主）

5. 因为他母亲病了，所以他没来参加春节晚会。（A跟B有关）

6. 我喜欢过春节，也喜欢过中秋节。（除了......以外，也/还......)

7. 他对这个工作很感兴趣，也很有信心，我们可以给他一个机会试试。
(既然......，那么[...]就.....)

阅读练习

中国人过年的风俗习惯很多跟吉利1的词语有关。比方说，过年时很多南方人有吃年糕的习惯。年糕本来写作粘2糕，是用糯米3做的，很粘，所以叫作粘糕。因为"粘"听起来像"年"，又非常好吃，而且过年时吃年糕，使人想到"年年高"、"一年比一年高"的意思，所以是很吉利的。中国人希望自己在新的一年里生活富足4，不但不缺5吃不缺穿，而且年年有余6，这就是为什么吃年饭时常有鱼、年画上也常画着鱼的缘故7。有的人还喜欢在过年期间吃发菜8。发菜看上去很像人的头发9，所以被叫作"发菜"。发菜味很美，同时也是祝愿10"发财"的意思。另外，过年时说话、做事也讲吉利，如果你不小心摔碎11了一个碗或者杯子，那么你应该马上说一句跟"碎"字有关的吉利话，如"岁岁平安12"，也就没事了。

过年时在香港13或者广东14，人们喜欢买一盆15小桔16树回家做装饰，树上结17着一个一个金黄色18的桔子，非常漂亮，象征19吉利。这是因为在广东话里"桔子"的"桔"跟"吉利"的"吉"发音20差不多，所以春节期间桔子也最受广东人喜爱。

除了这些风俗习惯以外，年画上画的东西也有很多跟吉利有关。比方说，有的年画上会画着蝙蝠21。你也许会不明白蝙蝠跟过年有什么关系。难道22蝙蝠也是吉利的吗？——一点不错23！因为"蝠"字跟"福24"字同音25！......说到26"福"字，可能有人又会问：为什么有时候看见贴在门上或者墙上的"福"字是倒27的？是不是贴错了？——哈哈，不是。这种贴法其实更有意思，因为说"福倒了！"的时候听起来就像说"福到了！"一样。这样说来，倒着贴的"福"不是更吉利吗？

生词表（请查出空着的词的意思）：

1. 吉利 [jílì] auspicious
2. 粘糕 [niángāo] sticky rice cake
3. 糯米 [nuòmǐ]__________
4. 富足 [fùzú]__________
5. 缺 [quē]__________
6. 余 [yú] surplus
7. 缘故 [yuángù] reason
8. 发菜 [fàcài]__________
9. 头发__________
10. 祝愿__________
11. 摔碎 [shuāi suì] drop and break
12. 岁岁平安__________
13. 香港 [Xiānggǎng] Hong Kong
14. 广东 [Guǎngdōng] Canton
15. 盆 [pén] pot (for plants)
16. 桔子 [júzi] oranges, tangerines
17. 结__________
18. 金黄色__________

19. 象征 [xiàngzhēng] symbolize　　20. 发音 ______________　　21. 蝙蝠 [biānfú] bats

22. 难道 Does that mean that... ?!　　23. 一点不错 ___________　　24. 福 [fú] blessing

25. 同音 _____________　　26. 说到 ______________　　27. 倒 [dào] upside-down

下面说的对不对？如果不对，是哪里不对？

1. 糯米做的食品很粘，所以很吉利。
2. 过年的时候吃鱼，意思是希望自己每年都有用不完的钱或者东西。
3. 发菜很好看，但是不好吃。
4. 过年期间摔碎东西是不吉利的事，所以得说一句吉利的话才好。
5. "岁岁平安"的意思是"年年平安"。
6. 广东人过年时买小桔树主要是因为好看，可以做装饰。
7. 因为蝙蝠代表的是不吉利的事，所以"福"字要倒着贴。
8. 这篇短文主要说的是中国人怎么过春节。

口语练习

I. 邀请客人常用语：（请练习两遍，第二遍试着说出来，不看书）

--我想请你春节到我家来吃饭，不知道你有没有空？（方便不方便？）

--这个星期天我们要包饺子吃，你能来吗？

接受邀请：哎呀，你太客气了，真不好意思。那什么时候来好？.

.....有什么需要我帮忙的吗？/还需要什么，我去买。

谢绝邀请：哎呀真对不起，我那天正好有点事，可能不能来了。下次吧。

II.情景会话

1.邀请人到家里来做客：请你和一个同学表演一下刘东请大为春节到家里去吃饺子的对话。

2.谈圣诞节和新年：如果你的中国朋友想知道西方人怎么过圣诞节(Shèngdànjié: Christmas)和新年，你怎么向他/她介绍？(可用下面〔写作练习〕里的图和词汇。)

III.叙述：你今年的新年或者春节是怎么过的？跟去年有什么不同？

写作练习

看图写作：把下面"过圣诞节和新年"写出来

有用的词汇：

商店 [shāngdiàn] store	大减价 [dà jiǎnjià] on sale	礼物 [lǐwù] gift
圣诞树 [shèngdànshù] Xmas tree	圣诞老人 Santa Claus	藏起来 [cáng qǐlai] to hide away
-前夕 [qiánxī] -eve	钟声 [zhōngshēng] sound of bell	"新年快乐" "Happy New Year"
拥抱 [yōngbào] to hug	亲吻 [qīnwěn] to kiss	

"礼多人不怪"

—做客—

第十一课

Situation	Structure	Culture
语言情景	语言结构	文化介绍

It's the second day into 春节 and 大为 has been invited to a friend's home. You'll join him as he finds out a bit about how to act when visiting a Chinese family.

In terms of grammar, you will look at the familiar words, 到 and 起来 , and discover new usages when those verbs combine with others to render some interesting patterns of expression.

And, culturally, as we said above, you will learn about the rules of etiquette that pertain between a host and a guest.

“礼多人不怪”

--做客--

(一)

春节的第二天，大为应邀到刘东家去做客。这是大为第一次到中国人家里去做客，他想，中国人说“礼多人不怪”，这说明中国人很重视礼貌，所以应该先问问刘东中国人在社交上[i]有些什么规矩。

大为： 刘东，你说我到中国人家做客的时候应该注意些什么？

刘东： 既然我们已经是朋友了，到我家来你就不必客气了。不过你要真想了解一点中国人的习惯的话，那有几点你应该注意一下。第一，跟异性在一起的时候千万别靠得太近，更不能拥抱亲吻。

大为： 这我注意到了，你们跟同性可以靠近，跟异性不可以。

刘东： 对了。第二，对老人、长辈得特别尊敬，说话别太随便，在称呼上也得注意一点儿。

大为： 那我应该怎么称呼你家里的人呢？

刘东： 你是我的好朋友，也跟我差不多大，那么我父母你可以称他们“刘伯伯”“刘伯母”。对其他人，可以用职务来称呼，比方说，“王医生”，“谢老师”，等等。

大为： 好在你告诉我，这对我太有用了，要不然又会闹笑话。真谢谢你！

刘东： 不谢。放心吧，你不会有问题的，中文说得这么棒！

大为： 谢谢！

i. 在...上...("in terms of .../as far as ... is concerned" or "in [the area of]... "). 在...上 is very commonly used and similar to 在...方面. However, 上, is not normally attached to 这 or 那 but it is correct to use 这 and 那 with 方面 Note the following examples:
在经济方面中国还不够强。（=在经济上：Economically,...）
在这方面我比你懂。(NOT: 在这上； BUT: 在这个问题上；在这件事情上)

礼	禮	lǐ	N rite, etiquette
礼多人不怪 禮多人不怪		lǐ duō rén bú guài	PH "You can't be too polite" (lit. "People don't blame you for being too polite")
做客		zuò//kè	VO to visit as an invited guest
应邀	應邀	yìngyāo	CV-O upon invitation ("respond to an invitation ")
说明	說明	shuōmíng	V to indicate
礼貌	禮貌	lǐmào	N (good) manners, courtesy
社交		shèjiāo	V/N to socialize; socializing
规矩	規矩	guīju	N norms, etiquette, unwritten rules
了解		liǎojiě	V to know well; to learn about
...的话	...的話	...dehuà	IE if...
异性	異性	yìxìng	N the opposite sex
千万	千萬	qiānwàn	A [colloq.] (Do/Don't...) by all/any means
靠		kào	V to lean against; to depend on
靠近		kàojìn	RV to get (physically) close to (sb. /sth.)
拥抱	擁抱	yōngbào	V to hold in arms, hug, embrace
亲吻	親吻	qīnwěn	V/N to kiss; kiss (colloq.: 亲)
尊敬		zūnjìng	V/N to respect (person); respect (to a person)
称呼	稱呼	chēnghū	V/N to address, call (also: 称); form of address
其他		qítā	SP other (people, things, places, etc.)
棒		bàng	ADJ [slang] super, excellent

刘东： 哈哈！这次你说错了。你应该说"哪里哪里，[ii]"听起来才像中国话，意思是"没有这回事"。

大为： 噢（O）！"哪里"原来是这个意思！...对了，我去做客应该带点什么才好？

刘东： 到我家就像到你自己家一样，什么都不必带。

大为： 你们不是说"礼多人不怪"吗？我带点葡萄酒来怎么样？

刘东： 那就随你便吧。对了，别来得太晚了啊！来晚了人家会以为你架子大！

大为： 真的？那我一定准时到！

（二）

刘东家里真热闹:老老小小一大家人，包饺子的包饺子、聊天的聊天。[iii]饺子熟了的时候，大为跟大家也熟了。刘东的母亲看见大为吃饺子吃得很开心，非常高兴，就对大为说:"大为啊，多吃点儿。今天我们没什么好菜[iv]，就包了点饺子，怠慢了[v]。"

大为没有学过"怠慢"这个词，所以没有听懂，以为说的是包饺子包得"太慢了"，就说:"不慢不慢。伯母，您包得快，我也吃得快，您看，我已经吃了这么多了，还慢吗？"大为说完，刘东一家人都笑了。

ii. "哪里" is an idiomatic expression abbreviated from "哪里的话" ("Where do these words come from?") or 哪里有这样的事? ("Where is there such a thing?"). It roughly corresponds to English "Not really" or "That's not true" or "Come on now" with a mild tone. It is used to deflect a compliment when the one complimented humbly refuses to take credit for a quality or action.

iii. "包饺子的包饺子，聊天的聊天。" (Lit. "Those who make dumplings make dumplings, those who chat chat" but really carrying the force of, "Some [of them] are making dumplings, while others are chatting.") This pattern can also be used to describe past events. Sentence A below focuses on an action, while sentence B with 了, emphasizes the result of an action.

A.那几个学生，出国的出国，工作的工作，都离开了北京。
Of those students, some went abroad and others started working. All left Beijing.

B. 那几个学生，出国的出国了，工作的工作了，都离开了北京。
Of those students, some have gone abroad, while others have found jobs (as planned). All left Beijing.

iv. "今天我们没有什么好菜" is a courtesy-expression conventionally used by the host at the outset of the meal.

v. "怠慢了" ("We have neglected/undertreated you" or "I'm being a poor host") is also a conventional phrase used by a host for courtesy purposes.

听起来	聽起來	tīng qǐlái	VP to sound [like..]
原来	原來	yuánlái	MA as it turned out, "so that's the reason for ..."
架子		jiàzi	N airs, haughty manner
架子大		jiàzi dà	IE put on airs; overbearing; insolent
准时	準時	zhǔnshí	ADJ/A on time, punctual; punctually
熟		shóu/shú	ADJ ripe, [food] cooked; familiar
开心	開心	kāixīn	ADJ happy, delighted
怠慢		dàimàn	V to neglect (a guest, senior, etc.)
词	詞	cí	N word, term

回答问题：

1.为什么大为要问刘东中国人社交方面的规矩？
2.刘东认为什么方面大为应该注意？
3.“哪里哪里”是什么意思？什么时候可以说？
4.为什么大为觉得去做客应该带点东西去？
5.为什么刘东叫大为不要去晚了？
6.“怠慢了”是什么意思？什么时候说这样的话？

语言结构

Focusing on Structure

I. Using Verb- 到

You have already seen 到 used as a suffix to verbs of movement/destination, as in,跑到，走到，送到，寄到, meaning "run to (a place), "walk to (a place), etc.到 can also be combined with other verbs, (in contrast to "movement verbs"), such as, 想、说、注意、了解 etc., to also denote arrival at or reaching a certain point (oftentimes unintentionally).

Examples:

你注意到没有：小王很喜欢小李。Have you noticed that Xiao Wang is attracted to Xiao Li.

我今天听到一件很奇怪的事。 I heard (by chance) a strange story today.

我没想到他会今天来。 It didn't occur to me that he would come today.

II. Using Verb-起来 to express some specialized meanings

You saw in Unit Four that 起来 is often attached to verbs or adjectives to express a newly occuring event or state with the meaning "start to..." or "start to get/become...." For example: 我学了两年日文，后来就学起中文来了 (After I studied Japanese for two years, I started learning Chinese).

We introduce another use of 起来 here. 起来 is often attached to an action verb (rather than an adjective), suggesting "when/by doing..." or "to do ...."

Examples:

这个歌听起来很熟。This song sounds familiar. (This song sounded familiar to me when I heard it.)

他看起来不像中国人。 He doesn't look (like) Chinese. (He doesn't look Chinese when you look at him.)

他的书读起来很有意思。 His books are fun to read. (His books are fun when read.)

这件事说起来容易做起来难。This job is easier said than done. (The job is easy when you talk about it but difficult when you do it.)

When 起来 is used with a verb-object, the format is: V起O来.. Example:

他爱玩儿，可是学起中文来也很努力。He loves to have fun, but he is really hardworking when studying Chinese.

词汇用法
Word Usage

Verbs

- 说明：说明情况(原因...)；请你说明一下你为什么这样做。/这件事说明了什么？/他一直没写信给你，说明他不喜欢你。
- 了解：了解一个人（一件事...）；了解一个人（一个地方）的情况；我对中国的情况非常了解。/我想了解一下你的生活（学习、工作...）情况。
- 靠：你们靠近一点。/靠得太近；椅子靠着桌子放。/他喜欢靠着窗户坐。
- 拥抱：我拥抱了他一下。/我们见面时很少互相拥抱。/他们拥抱在一起。
- 尊敬：尊敬老师；对长辈很尊敬；互相尊敬；他很受人尊敬。
- 称呼：我应该怎么称呼你？/我称呼他"老王"。/尊敬的称呼(N)

Verb-Object Compounds/Phrases

- 做客：到朋友家做客；做过一次客；做了三天客；做客做得很开心
- 闹笑话：他的英文不好，常常会说错话，结果闹过很多笑话。/闹了一个大笑话

Adjectives/Adverbs

- 熟：饭熟了。/水果还不熟。/我跟他很熟。/他对这个地方不熟。
- 开心：吃得很开心；我今天特别开心。/ 他拿了钱就开开心心地走了。
- 准时：来得很准时；他向来很准时。/飞机准时到达

Nouns

- 礼貌：懂礼貌；注意礼貌；他没什么礼貌。/这个小孩很有礼貌。/这样做不太礼貌(Adj.)。
- 社交：参加社交活动；他喜欢社交(V)。
- 规矩：社交上的规矩；他很懂规矩。/他没什么规矩。/他家里规矩很多。

Others

- ...的话：（如果）你学中文的话，那我也学。/你来的话，给我打个电话。
- 其他：其他〔的〕人（东西、事情、地方...）；我只喝茶，不喝其他饮料。/这些书，我喜欢这两本，其他的都没有意思。

句型和习惯用语

Sentence Patterns and Expressions

1.应邀到...来/去V **(come / go to...to do sth....upon invitation)**

- 大为应邀到刘东家去做客。
  Upon invitation, David went to Liu Dong's house as a guest.
- 张先生应邀到我们公司来参加晚会。
  Miss Li came to our company to see the performance upon invitation.

2.应该......才...... **(It's only [good,right,etc.]...for sb. to...)**

- 刘东告诉大为："你应该说'哪里哪里才像中国话。" Liu Dong told David: "You should say "Nali, Nali," and then it would sound more like Chinese."
- 这件事你应该先跟他商量商量才对。
- 明天到老师家做客，你说 ________________________________
- Since he left you a message, you should call him back.

3.在......上 **(in terms of...; in the area of...; -wise)**

- 中国人在社交上有些什么规矩？
  What norms do the Chinese people have in terms of socializing?
- 跟长辈说话时，在称呼上得注意一点。
- 他在学习上____________________, 可是在社交上____________________
- This country has huge problems economically.

4.千万(别)...... **(Do/Don't do......by all/any means!)**

- 他是开玩笑的，你千万别生气。He was just joking. Do not get angry,please!
- 自己一个人到国外去，千万要特别小心。
- 这件事我只告诉你一个人，你 ________________________________!
- Alcohol is not good for your health. By no means should you drink it.

5. ......，这说明......(**...it indicates that...; it tells you that...**)

- 中国人说“礼多人不怪”，这说明中国人很重视礼貌。 Chinese people say "You won't be blamed for being too polite." That indicates that Chinese people do value courtesy.
- 不管什么时候，她总是把家里收拾得干干净净的，这说明她是个很爱干净的人。
- 甲：我每次请他到家里来吃饭，他都说他没空。
  乙：____
- You helped him several times and he has never said a word of appreciation(一句感谢的话). That shows that he doesn't know what courtesy (demands).

6. V1的V1，V2的V2 (**...some are doing/did..., others are doing/did...**)

- 他家里很热闹，聊天的聊天，包饺子的包饺子。
- 我的学生这几天忙极了：买书的买书，考试的考试，上课的上课。
- 那几个人__________________________________，谁也不想看书。
- His children have all left home. Some went abroad; others got married.

7. ...V-起来... (**Sb. / Sth. is ... when ...; Sth. is ... to [do])**)

- 他看起来不像中国人。He doesn't look like a Chinese.
- 这个字念起来容易，写起来难。This word is easy to pronounce but difficult to write.
- 他很有经验，做起事来__________________________________。
- 我最喜欢______________，一___________起来就___________。
- He doesn't look smart, but he is very efficient when selling products.

- This sentence doesn't sound like Chinese.

文化介绍

Learning About Culture

做客时的规矩一主人和客人

When You're Invited to the Home of a Chinese Friend

What follows below are some considerations for you to keep in mind when you visit the home of a Chinese friend. Our description may be a bit on the idealistic side, maybe even old-fashioned, but, we think, useful, nonetheless.

On your arrival, the host will offer you tea, and, perhaps sweets or cigarettes. Now the offer of tea is a social ritual, expressing welcome for you. You should accept it, with both hands (showing respect), and have a few sips, even if tea is not your preferred drink. The point here is to show appreciation for the welcome. Next the children of the family will come in to greet you. The children will always be instructed by the parents to address you with an affectionate (but fictional) kinship term according to your status. For example, you may hear, 伯伯 bóbo (father's older brother) or伯母 bómǔ (father's older brother's wife), or 叔叔 shūshu (father's younger brother) or 阿姨 āyí (mother's sister). After the greeting, you might ask the children, 你几岁了？上学了没有？ or similar questions requiring very brief answers. After answering and, perhaps, asking about your health, the children will then leave or sit silently through the rest of the visit. Children are not expected to offer comments or contest the opinions of their elders. If you praise the children, the parents will immediately deflect the praise with some courtesy remark expressing that the ability of their children is not deserving of compliments.

After these opening formalities, a conversation follows naturally. You may expect questions about such topics as your studies, where you were originally from, your family, future plans, likes and dislikes, etc. Don't be surprised if your Chinese host is quite frank with his questions, asking, for example, how much money you made on your last job or your marital status!

Bringing a gift to your host or hostess is a good idea and a nice touch. It doesn't have to be anything elaborate, just something to show your friendship. One guide for you is that the value of the gift should vary according to the relationship between you and your host and the status of the host. Your Chinese host will accept your gift with thanks after some courtesy remarks but will usually not open it there and then, but rather put it to one side. This is not rudeness but rather is meant to show that the host is not "overeager" for the gift.

When the visit concludes, your host will normally ask you to stay on for lunch or dinner. If you decline and must leave, your host will see you to the front door to say good-bye and will remain there for a few moments, until you have left completely, again to show respect. In an apartment situation, it is not uncommon for your host to walk you to the elevator or even to the front door.

If you stay on for dinner, your Chinese friend will invariably start the meal by offering apologies for the insignificant number of dishes and their inferior quality, implying that the meal is unworthy of being served to you. Regardless of the number of dishes, which may run from four to six in an informal meal to ten or even twelve at a formal dinner, your host will usually remark, "There's not enough food. There's really nothing to eat."

The following expressions may prove useful when inviting or visiting a Chinese friend:

邀请（Inviting a friend):

李先生，我想请你星期天到我家来吃顿便饭。

接受邀请（ Accepting an invitation):

A close friend might accept with:

好极了！我正想跟你们聊一聊呢。不过千万别太麻烦。我带点什么来好？

If you're a new acquaintance, you might say:

哎呀，怎么好意思麻烦你们！

If you politely refuse, and your host insists, you might give in by saying:

好吧，那就麻烦你们了。你看我们什么时候来好？

谢绝邀请（Declining an invitation):

哎呀，真不巧！我有一点儿别的事要办。

OR

有一个朋友要来看我。

OR

家里还有好多事没办完。下次吧。谢谢了！

第十一课听力练习

第一部分：单句

请你们听下面的句子。每个句子的意思是什么？请在三个选择中选出一句来。

1. (a)甜的、油的东西对你的身体好。
(b)你想减肥就不应该常吃甜的、油的东西。
(c)你应该吃甜的、油的东西才能减肥。

2. (a)他有很多生活方面的问题，
(b)他在这里的生活过得很不好。
(c)他在这里的生活很顺利。

3. (a)我们对这件事没有看法。
(b)我们对这件事的看法差不多。
(c)我们对这件事的看法不一样。

4. (a)你参加晚会一定得准时。
(b)你迟到太久了，真不礼貌！
(c)参加晚会以前你应该先熟悉社交上的规矩。

5. (a)我到他的办公室和他聊天，感觉很轻松。
(b)他常常在办公室里看报、聊天，从这里可以看出他的工作很轻松。
(c)我想找一个可以让我看报、聊天的轻松的工作。

6. (a)新年的时候，我们都不愿意谈跟工作有关的事。
(b)新年的时候，我们一边玩一边还谈着跟工作有关的事。
(c)新年的时候，我们谁也不敢休息，还是谈着工作上的事。

第二部分：短文

第一遍:请你们听懂这篇短文的大意，然后回答问题。

问题：这篇文章主要在说些什么？
a)中国人的社交规矩　b)一次参加晚会的经验

第二遍:请你们读下面的句子，然后把这篇短文一段一段地再听一次。听完每一段后，看看每一个句子说得对不对。

第一段: _____ 这个人一到美国就很熟悉美国人的社交规矩了。

第二段: _____ 别的客人都在晚会开始以后才来。

第三段: _____ 她在晚会中认识了几个美国朋友，而且也学到了一些美国人的社交规矩。

第三遍:请你们读下面的问题，然后听第三遍。听完后，请回答问题。

1.那天的晚会，她为什么去得特别早？

2.主人见到她的时候怎么样？

3.晚会到什么时候才热闹了起来？

4.晚会中客人都做些什么？

5.晚会中有人说她衣服很好看，她怎么回答？

6.为什么到别人家里吃晚饭，一定得准时？

第十一课　练习

词汇；句型；语法

I.填空:

1.做客：我春节期间做______两次______。/上星期我________________去做______三天______。

2.规矩：________方面的规矩；/他们家的规矩________，所以我不喜欢去他家做客。中国人在__________上的规矩很多。/这个人很________。

3.礼貌：这个学生很________。/在中国，客人来了不倒茶是__________。

4.靠：你别________我。/他喜欢________________坐。/这两张画靠得太________，不好看。/把椅子__________放，这样方便一点。

5.了解：我没去过中国，所以不太了解中国的__________。/我今天来是想了解一下那个人的________________。/你__________他了解吗？

6.尊敬：中国人认为老人应该___________尊敬。/我________他很尊敬。

7.称呼：我应该______________称呼你？/他不喜欢人家____________他"____________"。/我喜欢"老李"、"小张"________________。

8.熟/熟悉：我跟他________。/我不__________美国的生活。/我________美国的生活很熟（悉）。/饭_________没有？/这个苹果还________________，一点也不好吃。

II.用适当的"V到"形式填空：(注意、看、受、想、谈、说、听)

a.我们今天开会的时候____________开春节晚会的事。

b.我今天在书店里__________一本很好的书，可是我的钱不够，没有买。

c.我刚___________他的事，他就来了。

d.他出国以后，我一直没____________他的情况。

e.这是一个很重要的问题，可是很多人都________________。

f.在中国老人比年轻人______更多的尊敬。在美国，老人常常_____尊敬。

g.在你决定做这件事的时候，有没有____________会有什么样的结果？

III.用“-起来”完成句子。注意“起来”在句子中的不同用法：

1.这支歌＿＿＿＿＿＿＿＿很像东南亚国家的。

2.他的样子＿＿＿＿＿＿是中国人，一听他说话才知道是日本人。

3.他学了一年中文后，接着又＿＿＿＿＿日文来了。

4.这个字＿＿＿＿＿＿＿容易＿＿＿＿＿＿＿难。

5.不知怎么搞的，她说着说着就＿＿＿＿＿＿＿＿＿＿了。

6.学生们开始只是在听音乐，听着听着就跟着音乐大声地＿＿＿＿＿。

7.他喜欢书，一＿＿＿＿＿＿＿＿＿就忘了吃饭睡觉。

8.刚开始的时候，我的字写得很不好看，现在好像＿＿＿＿＿＿＿了。

IV.改写下面的句子：

1.晚会上有的人唱歌，有的人跳舞，有的人聊天，有的人吃东西，热闹极了。(V的V)

2.他很少出去玩，从这里可以看出他对社交不感兴趣。（这说明......）

3.称呼自己亲戚和长辈的时候一定不能叫他们的名字。（千万......）

4.中国人过年过节时，在装饰方面常常以红色为主。（在......上）

5.他帮过我很多忙，这一次我如果不帮他的忙怎么行？（应该......才对）

6.他上星期接到一个邀请，于是去朋友家参加婚礼。（应邀到......去......）

阅读练习

谈"老"

不同的文化对"老"有不同的态度和看法。中国人传统上1尊老2，很注重辈分3，所以很多尊称4都有"老"字。比如说，称教书的人为"老师"，称年纪大的人"老大爷"，"老先生"，"老太太"等等。朋友之间5，为了表示6对对方7的尊敬常常会用"老李""老王"，或者"李大哥""王大姐"这样的称呼。如果称呼一个年老而又受大家尊敬的人，"老"字就得放在姓的后面听起来才更显得8尊敬：如"李老""王老"等等。小孩称呼父母的朋友时，也得按辈份来称：如果对方是比父母长一辈9的，那么就应该称对方"爷爷10""奶奶11"才对。

可是在其他一些国家，"老"字就不一定那么受欢迎了。有一次，一个不到五十岁的美国学者12到中国的一个幼儿园13去参观，他的头发14有一点灰白15。对中国人来说，头发灰白的人大多数是六十岁以上的人。所以他刚一进门，孩子们就很有礼貌地一起大声问候16："爷—爷—您—早！"在旁边的翻译17马上用英文解释18说："They say 'Good morning--Grandpa '"。这位学者听了以后，差一点大笑起来：他从来没想到会被人称作"Grandpa"。

还有一次，我认识了一位在美国的老华侨19，他已经七十多岁了，姓刘，是一个很受人尊敬的老人。按中国人的礼貌习惯，我尊称他"刘老"。可是这样称了几次以后，刘老对我说："以后别再称我'刘老'了。我知道你这样称呼是为了表示尊敬，可是我在美国的时间长了，已经不习惯这种称呼了。在美国，老字听起来很不舒服20，就跟'没用的人'、'快死的人'意思差不多。你还是叫我刘先生吧。"

生词表（查出或猜出空着的词语）：

1. 传统上________________
2. 尊老________________
3. 辈分 [bèifèn] seniority (in family, clan)
4. 尊称________________
5. ...之间 [zhījiān] among, between
6. 表示 [biǎoshì] to show (respect, love etc.)
7. 对方________________
8. 显得 [xiǎnde] to sound, seem
9. 长一辈________________
10. 爷爷 [yéye] grandpa
11. 奶奶 [nǎinai] grandma
12. 学者________________
13. 幼儿园 [yòuéryuán] nursery school, kindergarten
14. 头发________________
15. 灰白 [huībái] ashen, grey
16. 问候________________
17. 翻译 [fānyì] translator
18. 解释 [jiěshì] to explain, interpret
19. 华侨 [huáqiáo] overseas Chinese
20. 听起来很不舒服________________

回答问题：下面说的对不对？

1.按作者的看法，在中国文化里“老”字常常用来表示尊敬。

2.传统的中国人觉得辈分很重要，辈分大的人比辈分小的受尊敬。

3.“老李”和“李老”在称呼上是一样的，都是对老人的尊称。

4.幼儿园的孩子以为那位美国学者是一位老人，因为他的头发看起来像老人的。

5.那位姓刘的美国老华侨觉得他不应该受年轻人的尊敬。

6.姓刘的老人说他自己老了，是一个没用的人、快死的人了。

口语练习

I.练习下面的客套话：(一个人说，一个人答)

学生甲	学生乙
你好！	你好！
你好吗？/你怎么样？	还好。/还不错。/最近有点儿忙。
去哪儿？	去买点儿东西。/到学校去一下。
吃了没有？	还没呢，你呢？/吃了。你呢？
有空到我家来坐坐。	好的。/我会来的。你有空也到我那儿去玩。
来，跟我们一块儿吃饭吧。	不了不了。我已经吃过了/我还有事，马上就得走。
请坐，我去给你倒点儿茶。	别麻烦了，我坐一会儿就走。
今天没有什么好菜，随便吃一点儿。	您太客气了，这么多好吃的菜！
谢谢你给我们的礼物，让你花那么多钱。	这只是一点儿小意思，您别客气。
时间还早，再坐一会儿吧。	不（坐）了，你们该休息了。
我送你到门口。	您不必送了。请回吧。/请留步。
以后常来玩。	我会常来的。谢谢！再见。

你的中文说得真好！	哪里哪里，您过奖了。/还差得远呢。
我有一件事想向您请教一下。	不敢当！您请说。

II.情景会话：谈美国文化中的礼貌和客套话

有一个中国留学生刚到美国来，他不太熟悉美国人在社交方面的规矩，想请你告诉他应该注意些什么。（两个人一组，一个人问，一个人答。请先分别准备一下再开始练习。）

学生甲	学生乙
________________	________________
________________	________________
________________	________________
________________	________________
________________	________________
________________	________________

写作练习

1.前面的〔阅读练习〕短文里谈到中国人对老人和长辈的态度和习惯用语，你觉得跟你自己的文化习惯比起来有什么不同，请你用几个例子谈谈这个问题。

2.请看上面〔口语练习〕里的客套话例子，比较一下中国文化在礼貌和客套方面跟其他文化有些什么不同。

练习用下面的句子：

1.在......方面，中国人会......，因为中国人认为.......。而在同样的情况下，_____国人多半会......，因为____国人在......上很注重......，所以在......的时候会.......，意思是.......。

2.按......的习惯和规矩，在......的时候你（不）应该.......，这和______文化的习惯差不多/很不同。

3.比起来，____国文化更注意.......方面的规矩。比方说，.........。这说明.......。

4.不管你到哪个国家去，都应该了解那里的规矩，按那里的文化习惯做事。

“如果没有大为……”

—海琳见德生—

第十二课

Situation	Structure	Culture
语言情景	语言结构	文化介绍

You rejoin 海琳 at a rather unusual gathering of friends and relatives with marriage on their minds, the possible marriage of 海琳 and 德生, that is. And you get a chance to read not only their thoughts but those of 海琳 as well.

Grammatically, you'll take a look at the familiar verb 出来, when it is used to denote the result of action.

Culturally, you will learn about how Chinese parents approach perhaps the most important thing in their children's lives: 婚姻大事 ——— Marriage!

“如果没有大为……”

--海琳见德生--

春节伯母邀请赵太太一家来家里吃饭。赵家的儿子赵德生就是伯母要介绍给海琳的对象。吃饭时，大家一边谈话，一边也在想自己的心事。

（赵先生）

“海琳家跟我们家可以算是门当户对了，但不知道她人怎么样。看起来蛮懂规矩的，她跟德生好像也很谈得来，这我就放心了。唉（Ài），这个德生，都三十多的人了，一天只会读书，老让父母为他的婚事着急。这次要是再不行，那我们哪年哪月才能抱孙子啊？”

（赵太太）

“吴太太的这个侄女长得还不错，看上去也蛮聪明的，配我的德生嘛是可以了。不过她现在在一家什么大公司里做事，好像事业心很强，刚才还说以后还想上研究所。像她这样的人连忙自己的事都来不及，以后哪里[ii]还有时间照顾丈夫照顾家庭？哪里还会愿意做家务事？更别说生孩子带孩子了！对了，说不定她连孩子都不要呢，那可是万万[iii]不行！再说[iv]，有学问的女孩子动不动就[v]摆架子[vi]，那我可受不了！”

i. “看起来蛮懂规矩的” ("[She] appears to be well brought up.") 蛮 here suggests "to a considerable degree," similar to "rather...," "pretty...," in English. 的 is often attached to a 蛮-phrase to soften the tone.

ii.. “她哪里有时间.....？” ("How can she possibly have time to ...?") 哪里/哪儿 is used as a rhetorical question pattern. The literal meaning of this usage is "where does such a thing as ... exist?"
Examples:
这件事她哪儿会不知道？（她怎么会不知道？=她当然知道，一定知道）
他哪里是美国人？（他怎么会是美国人？=他根本不是美国人。）

iii. “万万不行” ("[It] won't do by any means!"). 万万 is a superlative used for emphasis. It is similar to the usage of 千万 except that 万万 can also be used in non-imperative sentences whereas 千万 cannot.
你万万不能做这件事！=你千万别作这件事。Don't you dare do this!
这种事他万万不会做。(not: 千万) Under no circumstances can he do this kind of thing!
我万万没想到她会跟他结婚！(not:千万) It never at all occurred to me that she would marry him!

赵	趙	Zhào	N (Chinese surname)
赵德生	趙德生	Zhào Déshēng	N (name of a person)
心事		xīnshì	N something weighing on one's mind
门当户对	門當戶對	mén dāng hù duì	PH a perfect match in social status (for marriage)
谈得来	談得來	tándelái	RV [colloq.] share common interest
都		dōu	A [colloq.] already
读	讀	dú	V to read, to study (sth.)
抱		bào	V to hold in arms, embrace
孙子	孫子	sūnzi	N grandchild
侄女		zhínü	N niece
蛮	蠻	mán	A [colloq.] quite, rather, pretty (good,etc.)
配		pèi	V to match
事业	事業	shìyè	N career, a pursuit
事业心	事業心	shìyèxīn	N ambition, devotion to one's pursuit
研究所		yánjiūsuǒ	N graduate/school institute (also 研究院)
来不及	來不及	láibují	RV [colloq.] cannot make it in time (to do sth.)
照顾	照顧	zhàogù	V/N to look after; care for; attend to
丈夫		zhàngfu	N husband
家庭		jiātíng	N family
更别说	更別說	gèng bié shuō	A let alone, to say nothing of
带孩子	帶孩子	dài háizi	VP to bring up a child,look after a child
对了	對了	duìle	IE [colloq.] By the way, ...; Oh yeah,
万万	萬萬	wànwàn	A by all/any means, under any circumstances
再说	再說	zàishuō	MA furthermore, besides
动不动就...	動不動就...	dòngbudòng jiù...	A (do...) too easily/frequently; always (ready to)...
摆	擺	bǎi	V to display; arrange
受不了		shòubuliǎo	RV can't tolerate or stand

（伯母）

"我早就知道海琳跟德生是再合适不过了。看看，两个人谈得不是蛮开心吗！海琳原来还不愿意见德生呢！.....欸（Éi)，赵太太怎么皮笑肉不笑的？看得出来她对海琳不那么满意。唉(Ài)，这个赵太太啊，就是老想找一个又漂亮又有文化[vii]又会做家务事的儿媳妇。哪里有这么十全十美的人呢？！她要不满意啊，那我还不愿意给她呢！"

（赵德生）

"这位吴小姐比我想像的可爱多了，虽然是从美国来的，可是没有什么架子，说起话来通情达理。不过听她的意思，她好像已经有男朋友了。这些老人们真是多事，何必非要给我们介绍对象不可呢？好在吴小姐人不错，跟她交个朋友也好。希望她对我也有好感。"

iv. "再说，..." ("Besides/In addition/What's more,...") is very commonly used to buttress a final point. Here are some examples:
他没有工作， 再说，他也不住在北京，所以我没有跟他结婚。
我不喜欢那里：人又多，房租又贵。再说，学校也不好。
But note in this example how 再说 differs from 而且：他很有钱，而且（ not 再说！）他也很聪明。

v. "动不动就...." ("at the slightest provocation/be apt to; at every turn") Examples:
你这几天怎么动不动就生气？ How come you get mad so easily these days?
你别动不动就吃药。 Don't take medication whenever you feel like it!

vi. 摆架子 (bǎi jiàzi) means "put on airs"/"think who the heck you are"

vii. "有文化的人", literally "those having culture" but really meaning "a literate person." It often refers to people with higher education, i.e. above the high school level. You can also say 没有文化 to mean "illiterate", or 有一点文化 "can read and write [to some extent]".

儿媳妇	兒媳婦	érxífu	N daughter-in-law
十全十美		shí quán shí měi	PH (of a person or thing) perfect, good in every aspect
想象	想像	xiǎngxiàng	V/N to imagine; imagination
可-		kě-	BF -able, -ible
可爱	可愛	kě'ài	ADJ lovable, cute
通情达理	通情達理	tōng qíng dá lǐ	PH (of a person) understanding and reasonable
多事		duōshì	V meddlesome
何必		hébì	QW [rhetorical] What's the point...? (It's not necessary...)
非...不可		fēi...bùkě	IE must; insist on
好感		hǎogǎn	N good impression or feelings (about a person)

判断出以下词语的意思：

婚事
家务事　　　家務事
皮笑肉不笑

（海琳）

"我原来以为德生是个眼镜片有啤酒瓶底那么厚、一天到晚只会看书的书呆子，哪知道[viii]人家根本不是我想像的那个样子，而且说起话来蛮有趣的。听得出来他很有学问，看上去也很体贴人，跟这样的人在一起真轻松。要是没有大为，说不定……"

原来	原來	yuánlái	ADJ/MA original, initial; originally, initially
眼镜	眼鏡	yǎnjìng	N eye-glasses
眼镜片	眼鏡片	yǎnjìngpiàn	N. eye-glass lens
瓶		píng	M/N bottle, jar
厚		hòu	ADJ (of flat objects) thick
书呆子	書呆子	shūdāizi	N bookworm, nerd (lit. "book idiot")
根本		gēnběn	A at all
有趣		yǒuqù	ADJ interesting, amusing
学问	學問	xuéwèn	N knowledge, learning
体贴	體貼	tǐtiē	V be considerate (of others' needs, feelings)

回答问题：
1.赵先生觉得海琳怎么样？他愿意不愿意海琳做他的儿媳妇？
2.赵太太喜欢海琳吗？她有些什么想法？她愿意海琳做儿媳妇吗？
3.海琳的伯母有什么想法？
4.德生原来想像中的海琳是什么样的人？他现在的看法呢？
5.海琳喜欢德生吗？德生跟她原来想像的有什么不同？
6.如果你是德生，你会怎么想？如果你是海琳，你应该爱德生还是爱大为？

viii. "哪知道…." ("[but] it turned out to my surprise that..." or "but I was surprised to find out that...")
Example:
我想他会下星期走，哪知道他昨天就走了。I thought that he would leave next week, but, to my surprise, he left yesterday.

语言结构

Focusing on Structure

Using Verb-出来 with Non-Directional Verbs

You've learned that the resultative ending 出来 is used with verbs like拿 (so拿出来) to suggest 'direction out.' Similarly, when attached to non-directional verbs, 出来 suggests that something has been detected, figured out, or made obvious from a source through doing something. Consider the following examples:

听出来	detect/find out through/by listening
看出来	find out/discern through seeing/observing
想像出来	visualize by imagining
检查出来	discover after inspection/examining
研究出来	find out through research/study

Here are some more examples. Note how the negative is formed (看不出来) and how Verb-出来 behaves when the negative is combined with an object:

我(从他的话里)听出来他对中文很有兴趣。	I can tell from how he talks that he is interested in Chinese.
从她皮笑肉不笑的样子上我看出来她不喜欢海琳。	I know from her phony smile that she doesn't like Helen.
听他的声音，我想像不出他的样子来。	Just by listening to his voice, I can't imagine what he looks like.
医生没有检查出我的病来。	After the tests/examination, the doctor didn't discover what my illness was.

Note the difference between V-出来 and V-起来 (see previous unit). Compare:

1a.他说话听起来像日本人。	His speech sounds like Japanese.
1b.我听出来他是日本人。	I can tell that he is Japanese from his speech/accent.
2a.他看起来很有经验。	He looks very experienced.
2b.我看出来他很有经验。	I know by observing him that he is very experienced.
3a.这种病检查起来很难。	This disease is difficult to examine. (The examination process is difficult.)
3b. 这种病检查出来很难。	This disease is difficult to detect.

词汇用法

Word Usage

Verbs

- 照顾：照顾孩子；照顾别人的需要；好好地照顾照顾身体；照顾得很好；他给了我很多照顾。/谢谢你对我们的照顾(N)。
- 读：读书（报、小说）；这本书我读过三次；他在大学读书（读中文、读音乐）。/读了四年大学（研究所）；我是读语言学的，你是读什么的？
- 配：配一配颜色(菜、家具、衣服...)；配得很好；你也喜欢经济学，你配他正好。/这个菜的颜色配得很漂亮。/白色配什么颜色都好看。
- 想像：你想像一下我的感觉(心情、样子...)。/他比我想像的老多了。/我们十多年没见面了，真想像不出来你现在的样子。
- 体贴：她很体贴人。/对他体贴得不得了；他对人很体贴(Adj.)。
- 抱：抱着孩子(几本书、一大包东西)；把书抱在手里；孩子太重，我抱不动。
- 带（孩子）：她又工作又带孩子，很辛苦。/带过三个孩子；把孩子带大了

Resultative Verb Expressions

- 谈得\不来：你跟他谈得来谈不来？/我们兴趣差不多，所以很谈得来。
- 来得\不及：八点的晚会我们来得及来不及参加？/我们现在去还来得及。/我刚才很忙，来不及给你打电话。
- 受得\不了：你受得了受不了这里的天气(这个人、这种态度...)？

Adjectives/Adverbs

- 有趣：这个人(这本书、这个电影、这门课...)很有趣；我昨天看了一本很有趣的书。
- 蛮：蛮有礼貌(漂亮、聪明、流利...)的；蛮懂规矩的；这家餐厅装饰得蛮漂亮的。
- 根本：他说他懂英文，其实他根本不懂。/他根本没学过英文。/她根本不会开车。
- 都：他都三十岁了，还没对象。/都八点了，快回家吧。/都快考试了，他还在玩。

Nouns/Noun Phrases

- 心事：想心事；他有很多心事。/找对象这件事一直是我最大的心事。
- 家庭：他有一个很大的家庭。/他很关心（照顾...）家庭。/他家的家庭关系很好。
- 文化：中国文化；在文化上...；他的文化很高。/他很有文化。/有文化的人(Adj.)
- 学问：他的学问很深(很高)。/做菜的学问很大。/他很有学问(Adj.)。
- 像...这样的...：像这样的人；像他这样的人；像他这样热情的人；像他这样努力学中文的人；像北京大学这样(有名)的学校；像"老李""小王"这样的称呼

Idioms/Set Phrases

- 门当户对：你们两家门当户对。/他们两家门不当户不对，可是他们还是要结婚。
- 通情达理：这个人很通情达理，所以我喜欢他。/她说话、做事一点都不通情达理。
- 十全十美：对我来说，这个人（这件衣服、这所房子...)十全十美。/这件事做得十全十美。/生活中哪里有十全十美的事？

句型和习惯用语

Sentence Patterns and Expressions

1. V出O来;V出来 **+ clause (Sb. detects ... through doing...)**

- 我（从他的语气里）听出他的意思来了。
  I knew what he really meant (from his tone).
- 我看得出来你有心事。
- 医生给他检查了三次，可是 ______________________________________。
- A: Can you tell who wrote these words? B: It looks like David's writing.

2. ...非（要）......不可 **(Sb. must do...\ Sb. insists on...)**

- 如果想说好中文，你非每天练习不可。
  If you want to be fluent in Chinese, you must practice every day.
- 今天天气不好，可他非要今天去不可。
  The weather is bad today, but he insists on going there today.
- 他这个人真奇怪，为什么非要我 ______________________________不可？
- A: It looks like you must go [there] today.
  B: But why me (Why must I be the one to go)?! Why must it be today?!

3. (Sb.\Sth.)哪(里)......？**(Rhetorical: How can it be the case that...?)**

- 她每天都那么忙，哪(里)有时间照顾家庭？ She is so busy every day. How does she manage to find the time to take care of her family?
- 像他那样的人，哪(里)愿意做家务事？
- 中文哪里像他说的那样 ____？
- How could she possibly be my girl friend?! How on earth do I have a girl friend?!

4. (连)...都...，更别说...了 **(even......, let alone......)**

- 快考试了，我连饭都来不及吃，更别说跟你出去玩了！ The finals are coming soon. I don't even have the time to eat, not to mention going out with you!
- 他连这么简单的字都不会写，更别说难一点的字了。
(or:他连这么难的字都会写，更别说简单一点的字了。)
- 她这几天肚子不太舒服，连牛奶都不能喝，______________________________
- He didn't even go to an ordinary college, let alone a top school like Beijing University.

5. .....，再说...也......，所以......**(.... besides,..., so......)**

- 他没有这方面的工作经验，再说，他也不会用电脑，所以我们不能雇用他。
- 他上课常常迟到，再说，他也不努力，所以老师不喜欢他。
- 他现在没什么钱，____
- That area is not very quiet. Besides, the rent there is also high, so I don't want to live there.

6. 动不动就V **..... (VP at the slighest provocation/at every turn/ easily/ frequently *[remember this form implies something negative]*)**

- 你怎么动不动就生气？How come you get mad over nothing?!
- 这个地方动不动就下雨，真讨厌！
Every time you turn around it's raining around here. It's really a pain!
- 他动不动就 ____，我真是受不了！
- He is always ready to tell people that he's got money.

7. 万万...；万万别...；万万没想到...(... under no circumstances/ by no means)

- 你万万不能做这件事！ Under no circumstances should you do this!
- 我万万没想到他会被那个公司雇用。(not interchangable with 千万)
- 甲：说不定她连孩子都不要呢！乙：________________________________
- Please by no means tell him about this!

8. 何必......(呢)？(Rhetorical: Why bother about...? \ Why should\must...?)

- 他是开玩笑的，你何必认真？He is just joking, why do you have to take it personally?
- 表演三点才开始，我们何必去那么早？
- 到我家来，________________________________
- Since she's already told you she doesn't love you any more, why do you still bother calling her every day?

9. 我以为......哪知道...... (I had thought/had assumed..., but I was surprised to find that...)

- 我以为他什么都不懂，哪知道他其实很有学问。
  I thought he was quite ignorant, but to my surprise, he is actually very knowledgeable.
- 我以为他是一个只会看书的书呆子，哪知道完全不是这样。
- ________________________________，哪知道其实很容易。
- 我以为他常常出国，________________________________
- I thought they would get along well. But, to my surprise, it's actually not the case.

文化介绍

Learning About Culture

中国人的传统婚事

Chinese Traditions About Marriage

Chinese parents are uncommonly anxious about their children's marriages. For parents, marriage is vital because it insures the continuity of the name of the family/clan. Centuries ago, the Chinese Confucian philosopher, Mencius, (孟子, Mèng zǐ) taught that "Of the three things that are unfilial, to have no progeny is the greatest of these." This idea is still alive in the Chinese mind today. To Chinese parents, to have an unmarried child in the family is the greatest regret of their life. Thus, to see a son or daughter married is a serious parental duty. Even in today's China, parents may use a matchmaker to find the most appropriate spouse for their child.

Once the young man/woman finds a possible mate, with or without his or her approval, family conferences are held to discuss the matter. In addition to personal qualifications, another important aspect considered is mén dāng hù duì 门当户对 (literally, matching the door), that is to say, making certain that the social and economic status of the two families is comparable. Ideally, at least in the mind of the parents, a good husband should be well-behaved, respectful, have a good education, be ambitious, and have prospects for a bright future. Physical appearance is secondary, as long as the young man has no abnormality. An ideal prospective wife, has, of course, different qualities. Ambition, career prospects, and the like, are less important than personal appearance. A very important quality is her ability to be a good housewife and help advance her husband's future career.

In the past, when the marriage-match had finally been decided, families would invite relatives and friends to an engagement party. Preparations for the marriage now seriously began. Since daughters were usually given a dowry at the time of their marriage, parents now began to assemble one. A dowry usually consisted of household articles, clothes and jewelry.

Chinese are traditionally color-conscious. Since red is the color of happiness, it is an important color motif for the wedding. For example, wedding invitations are most often printed on red paper with Chinese characters written in gold. Red is also prominent in the bride's clothing, except for that worn during the actual marriage ceremony, when brides often wear white due to the influence of the West.

The wedding ceremony can take place wherever the parents choose -- in a church (in Taiwan), at home or even at a restaurant. After the ceremony, the bride and groom -- assuming they are young -- generally go to a photographer's studio where, wearing their wedding outfits, they pose for the usual photographs. After these formalities, a banquet is given in a fine restaurant. Many brides change out of their wedding gowns into fancy dresses (sometimes several times!) during the banquet.

One last word about a traditional Chinese wedding: the groom's family pays for it, and the money often includes support for the wife until the groom is well established financially.

第十二课听力练习

第一部分：单句

请你们听下面的句子。每个句子的意思是什么？请在三个选择中选出一句来。

1. (a)他是个聪明的孩子，学习起来应该很顺利。
(b)他的学习有问题，因为他不够聪明。
(c)他是个聪明的孩子，何必太认真学习呢？

2. (a)他不是个通情达理的人。
(b)他在什么事情上通情达理？
(c)他也许是个通情达理的人。

3. (a)小张认为王小姐是个十全十美的女孩。
(b)王小姐聪明漂亮，可是小张还是觉得不够满意。
(c)小张觉得李小姐比王小姐好。

4. (a)那个公寓虽然小一点儿，但很便宜，所以我打算租下来。
(b)我不愿意租那个公寓，因为我对客厅和附近的环境都不满意。
(c)除了客厅太小以外，那个公寓其实没什么不好。

5. (a)这个孩子不小了，为什么常常要人抱他？
(b)这个孩子还小，需要常常抱着他。
(c)这个孩子不爱运动，喜欢人家抱他。

6. (a)有礼貌的人千万不能做这种事情。
(b)他做出这种事使我们觉得非常奇怪。
(c)我们想象不出来他多么有礼貌。

7. (a)我现在才知道原来他并不受人欢迎。
(b)我不知道大家对他有没有好感。
(c)我听说大家都很喜欢他。

第二部分：短文

第一遍:请你们听懂这篇短文的大意，然后回答问题。

问题：这个母亲希望她的女儿怎么样？

a)赶快跟一个好对象结婚

b)赶快成为一个医生

第二遍:请你们读下面的句子，然后把这篇短文再听一次。听完后，请在这个母亲可能会同意的句子旁边打勾。(Place a check next to the statements that the mother in this story would agree with.)

_____1.女儿已经不小了，该结婚了。

_____2.女儿不结婚没关系，只要她过得快乐就好了。

_____3.女儿现在有一个很好的男朋友。

_____4.女儿刚认识的这个医生是一个很合适的对象。

_____5.世界上没有十全十美的人。.

第三遍:请你们读下面的句子，然后把这篇短文一段一段地再听一次。听完后，看看这些句子说得对不对。

第一段:

_____1.这个人的女儿虽然只有大学学历，可是人很聪明能干。

_____2.她女儿现在是一家进出口公司的秘书。

_____3.她女儿觉得事业比较重要。

_____4.她和她先生都希望女儿能结婚，这样他们才能抱孙子。

第二段:

_____1.她女儿从以前到现在都没有男朋友。

_____2.她女儿不满意别人给她介绍的对象。

第三段:

_____1.最近有人为她女儿介绍一个又有礼貌长得又帅的医生。

_____2.她觉得这个医生和她的女儿很配。

_____3.她女儿跟这个医生谈不来。

第十二课　练习

词汇；句型；语法

I.<u>填空</u>：

1.<u>学问</u>：他有____________方面的学问。/我的朋友很______________。

2.<u>配</u>：_________配__________正好。/我觉得他配不______你。/________配_______不合适。

3.<u>照顾</u>：我不在家的时候，她常常帮我__________。/谢谢你______他的照顾。他现在身体很好，不需要_________照顾。

4.<u>蛮</u>：你的男朋友蛮_____________。/这张桌子蛮_________。/他的中文说得_____________。

5.<u>想象</u>：我真想象_________你现在是什么样子。/我想象我的对象_________________________的人。

6.<u>像…的N</u>：像北京大学_____________；像_______________的事；像IBM那样的__________；像老李那样__________的人；我想住在________________那样________的地方。

II.<u>用“V-起来”还是“V-出来”</u>？

1.我只说了一次，他就听_______我的意思来了。

2.你的声音听______像北京人。/我听____________他是哪国人。

3.他看______只有三十岁；谁也没看________他其实已经有四十多岁了。

4.我写完作文以后好好地检查了一下，可是没______________什么错。

5.这种病检查_________很容易，可是医________就很难了。

6.我一点也想象__________他一个人在中国怎么过。

7.他_______________架子蛮大的，可是________________什么都不行。

（说话，做事）

III.下面的句子是什么意思？（请选出正确解释）

1. “我万万没有想到大为会爱上海琳。”　　意思是：
   a.我想来想去，还是不明白为什么大为会爱上海琳。
   b.我从来没有想到过大为会爱上海琳。

2. “你万万不能一个人到那个地方去。”　　意思是：
   a.不管怎么样，你都不能一个人到那里去。
   b.你去几次可以，但不能去很多次。

3. “我看他很有礼貌，哪知道他是一个坏人！”意思是：
   a.他虽然很有礼貌，但我看出来他不是个好人。
   b.他看上去很有礼貌，所以我没有看出来他其实是个坏人。

4. “你这几天怎么动不动就喝酒？”　　意思是：
   a.你这几天喝酒的次数太多了。　　b.你这几天为什么一运动就喝酒？

5. “他哪里对这个感兴趣？”　　意思是：
   a.他对这个根本不感兴趣。　　b.他在什么地方对这个感兴趣？

6. “我看不出来你是这个公司的经理。”　　意思是：
   a.看你的样子，我不知道你是这个公司的经理。
   b.你看起来像这个公司的经理，其实不是。

7. “如果你想学好中文，就非天天练习不可。”　　意思是：
   a.你得天天练习才行。　　b.你不必天天练习。

8. “他连自己的事都做不好，更别说帮别人的忙了。”意思是：
   a.他如果做不好自己的事情，就不应该说帮别人的忙。
   b.如果他连自己的事都做不好，哪里能帮别人的忙？

9. “电影七点才开始，我们何必这么早就去？”意思是：
   a.我们不必去那么早。　　b.我们应该不应该这么早就去？

10. “他非要自己一个人去不可。”意思是：
   a.他觉得自己一个人去不行。
   b.他觉得他一定要自己一个人去。

阅读练习

是谁的错？

有一本杂志上说了一对夫妻1的事。刚结婚的时候丈夫2没有什么事业心，每天下班以后不是跟朋友喝茶聊天，就是在家看报纸看电视。可是妻子希望丈夫是一个成功3的男人，一个在事业上有成就4的男人，于是就鼓励5丈夫在事业上发展。丈夫听了妻子的话，开始努力发展事业，每天都在外面忙，家里的事全都让妻子一个人管。妻子又上班、又管家务、又带孩子，很辛苦。可是看着丈夫在事业上有了进步，她自己心里很高兴，一点也不抱怨6。慢慢地丈夫越来越不关心家里的事了，晚上回来得也越来越晚了，而且周末7也常出去，说有公务8要办。妻子想，丈夫正在一步9一步地走向成功，当然应该支持10他，自己做出牺牲11是应该的，值得12的。丈夫的事业越做越大，很快成了一个有钱有势13的人，忙得跟妻子见面的时间都很少了。终于14有一天，丈夫向妻子提出15："我们离婚16吧"。妻子一听呆了17，傻傻地站在那里说不出话来。丈夫接着说："我的心已经给了别人了"。这时候妻子才明白丈夫是有了外遇18，而这位第三者19就是他公司里的年轻漂亮的公关20小姐！

有人说这个丈夫太没有良心21了：如果没有太太的鼓励和支持，他哪里会有什么成就？更别说有今天的钱和势了！也有人说这个家庭悲剧22应该怪妻子，因为一开始她爱的就不是本来23的他，而是她想像中的一个有成就的他。因为她非要丈夫出去发展事业不可，当然丈夫也就离她越来越远，而爱上一个每天跟他一起工作、谈得来的人。所以丈夫有了婚外恋24 不是丈夫的错。还有人认为，如果妻子自己也在事业上有发展，那么丈夫不会跟她离婚。你的看法呢？

生词表（查出空着的词的意思）

1.夫妻 [fūqī] husband and wife	2.丈夫 [zhàngfu] husband	3.成功 ______________
4.成就______________	5.鼓励 [gǔlì] encourage	6.抱怨 [bàoyuàn] complain
7.周末 [zhōumò] weekend	8.公务 [gōngwù]__________	9.步 [bù]______
10.支持 [zhīchí]__________	11.牺牲 [xīshēng] sacrifice	12.值得 [zhíde] worthwhile
13.势 [shì]___________	14.终于 [zhōngyú] finally	15.提出 ___________
16.离婚______________	17.呆了 [dāi] stupified	18.外遇 [wàiyù]_____
19.第三者 ___________	20.公关 (=公共关系)	21.良心 [liángxīn] conscience
22.悲剧 [bēijù] tragedy	23.本来 ______________	24.婚外恋 _______

回答问题：下面说的对不对？如果不对，哪里不对？

1.丈夫结婚以前没有什么成就，因为他的能力比较差。

2.刚结婚的时候，他下了班不喜欢跟朋友聊天，只喜欢看报纸、电视。

3.妻子希望有一个有钱的丈夫，所以要丈夫多工作，少看电视。

4.妻子虽然不高兴丈夫很晚才回家，周末又出去办事，但还是愿意支持丈夫。

5.丈夫工作太忙，所以很少跟妻子见面。

6.妻子根本没想到丈夫会提出离婚。

7.有人认为丈夫的成功是妻子鼓励支持的结果，所以丈夫根本不应该提出离婚。

8.也有人认为妻子应该对离婚的事负责，因为她自己太不关心丈夫的事业了。

9.还有人认为妻子应该跟丈夫在一起工作，一起在事业上发展。

口语练习

I.练习以下习惯用语：

A.用“哪里”句回答：

例：A:听说王先生是搞经济学的。B:他哪里是搞经济学的？他是搞进出口的。

1.小李说他在一家大公司工作。
2.他们俩好像很谈得来。
3.你怎么动不动就生气？
4.中国字看起来难，写起来很容易。
5.你真是一个书呆子！
6.你的女朋友/男朋友怎么没来？

B.用“连.....都...,更别说......了”回答：

例：A:小王怎么没有去上课？　B:他连学校都没回，更别说去上课了！

1.你要上研究院了吗？
2.她不愿意做家务事吗？
3.你去中国留过学没有？
4.你怕不怕坐飞机？

C. 用"哪知道……"完成句子：

1. 我以为他是中国人，哪知道＿＿＿＿＿＿＿＿＿＿＿＿＿＿＿＿。

2. 他告诉我他下星期才走，哪知道＿＿＿＿＿＿＿＿＿＿＿＿＿＿。

3. 我想他一定是上课去了，哪知道＿＿＿＿＿＿＿＿＿＿＿＿＿＿。

4. 他们上星期刚结婚，哪知道＿＿＿＿＿＿＿＿＿＿＿＿＿＿＿＿。

II. 讨论："到底是谁的错？"（请先看本课〔阅读练习〕）

1. 对话练习：（请两人一组，按下面的情景表演出妻子和丈夫的对话）

a. 妻子说服丈夫应该做一个有事业心、有成就的男人

b. 丈夫向妻子提出离婚

2. 谈看法：你认为是丈夫的错还是妻子的错？你同意别人的看法吗？为什么？

练习用下面的词汇和句式：

我（不）同意＿＿的看法（做法）。

按＿＿的说法（看法），……好象应该……才对。

在我看来，……/我认为……应该是……

我不明白为什么……

这样做是为了……，所以我（不）认为这件事应该怪＿＿＿。

写作练习

写讨论概要、谈自己的看法：

上面的口语练习中讨论了"到底是谁的错"这个题目。现在请你先把讨论中别的同学的看法概括(gàikuò: summarize)一下，然后谈谈你的看法。

练习用下面的句子：

我们今天对"到底是谁的错"这篇文章作了一次讨论。讨论中大家有不同的看法。有的人认为……，因为……。也有的人不同意这种看法，认为……。还有的人说……。我的看法是……比如说，……，难道这样做……？所以我认为……。

“龙到底是怎么来的？”

—讨论龙的神话—

第十三课

Situation 语言情景 **Structure** 语言结构 **Culture** 文化介绍

In this lesson you join 大为 in a discussion with his teacher about a topic that interests him greatly: where do dragons come from? Although this sort of inquiry sounds rather juvenile, it is important because the motif and the lore about dragons is so prominent in Chinese culture. You will learn a bit about dragons but, more importantly, practice language useful when discussing an issue.

Grammatically, you'll focus on two forms:
using 不是 ...吗 in a rhetorical question-- and
using 作 as a suffix to verbs to create lots of expressions.

Just as many in the West believe in astrology, so do many Chinese. So, in terms of culture, you will look into the Chinese version of the horoscope, which involves twelve animals, (十二生肖，shēngxiào), rather than nine planets. In the process you'll get to appreciate some things that the East and the West share.

“龙到底是怎么来的？”

--讨论龙的神话--

春节期间大为看了一些表演，也参观了博物馆，他印象最深的是中国人对龙的崇拜。龙在中国人的生活中可以说无处不在[i]：房屋上、博物馆里、年画上、装饰物上都有龙的形象，春节时到处也都在表演龙舞。龙在中国文化里为什么受到这么大的重视呢？大为对这个问题很感兴趣。

大为：王老师，据我所知，自然界里虽然曾经有过恐龙，但并没有龙这种动物，那么中国文化中的龙到底是怎么来的呢？

王：这是个很复杂的问题，很多学者都对龙的神话做过研究，可是到现在还没有一个统一的看法。有的人说，龙的形象跟闪电很相似，认为龙的神话可能是古代的人对自然现象不理解的结果：看见闪电，接着就打雷、下雨、发大水[ii]，所以就把闪电看作是神的出现，后来就把它叫作龙了。

i. “无处不在”（lit. "no place [it] is not present"--It is everywhere.）无...不...is a double negative form conveying a strong positive. 无 ("no") has a classical or literary flavor and should be matched with a comparable lexical item if there is one. It is typically followed by a monosyllabic word. Examples:
他无恶不做。(恶 :=坏事）There's no evil [thing] that he doesn't do.
他无书不看。 He reads everything.

ii. 闪电、打雷、下雨、发大水, etc. are all verb phrases for natural phenomena which do not need (like English) to prepose a formal subject, (e.g. *It* is raining.)

讨论	討論	tǎolùn	V/N to discuss (issues); discussion
龙	龍	lóng	N dragon
神话	神話	shénhuà	N legend, myth
参观	參觀	cānguān	V/N to tour, visit (a place); tour, visit
博物馆	博物館	bówùguǎn	N museum
印象		yìnxiàng	N impression (on one's mind)
深		shēn	ADJ deep
崇拜		chóngbài	V/N to worship, idolize; worship
无	無	wú	A [lit] no, without (=没有)
无处不在	無處不在	wú chù bú zài	PH ubiquitous
-物		wù	BF object, thing (used as N-Suf.)
动物	動物	dòngwù	N animal
形象		xíngxiàng	N image
据	據	jù	CV according to, based on
据...所知	據...所知	jù...suǒzhī	VP according to what sb. knows
-界		-jiè	SUFF world, field, circle (自然界,报界)
恐龙	恐龍	kǒnglóng	N dinosaur
复杂	複雜	fùzá	ADJ complicated, complex
学者	學者	xuézhě	N scholar
统一	統一	tǒngyī	V/N to unify; uniformity,unification; unity
闪电	閃電	shǎn//diàn	V/N to have lightning; lightning
相似		xiāngsì	ADJ similar
古代		gǔdài	TW ancient times
现象	現象	xiànxiàng	N phenomenon, sign
雷		léi	N thunder
打雷		dǎ//léi	VO to thunder
发大水	發大水	fā dàshuǐ	VP to flood
出现	出現	chūxiàn	V/N to appear, emerge; appearance, emergence
它		tā	N it (used for animals etc.)

大为：您同意这种说法吗？

王：我觉得另一个学者的说法更有道理。这个学者认为龙的神话跟古代的部落崇拜动物有关。中国古代很多部落都用一种动物来[iii]做自己部落的象征，有的是蛇，有的是马，有的是鹿，有的是鸟等等。当这些部落统一以后，就把各种动物的特点集中在一起，这样就有了龙。这就是为什么龙有蛇身、马头、鹰爪、鹿角，能在天上飞也能在水里游的缘故。由于龙无所不能[iv]，代表着最高权力，另外，据有的学者研究，龙又是中国第一个朝代夏朝的象征，所以中国的皇帝都把自己称作龙，中国人也常常把自己比作龙的子孙。

大为：怪不得我在博物馆里看到的皇帝的床、衣服等等都是用龙的形象来做装饰的。对了，还有一点我不太明白：中国人爱说[v]"望子成龙"，这句话是什么意思？

王：噢（O），这是一个成语，意思是希望孩子长大以后成为一个有能力、做大事的人。欸(Éi)，对了，西方不是也有龙的神话吗？下次上讨论课的时候你能不能谈谈西方的龙跟中国的龙有什么不同？

大为：好，我觉得这个题目很有意思。

王：我想大家也一定会很感兴趣的。

iii. "用一种动物来做自己部落的象征" ("...use [the image of] an animal to serve as an emblem of the tribe"). 用......来......(use...to [do sth. or serve the purpose of sth.]) is used often in Chinese. Note that the 用-phrase suggests the means and 来 introduces the purpose. Typically, the means and purpose in this usage are not directly related. (If the means is directly related to the purpose,来 is usually omitted. E.g. 用筷子吃饭,用中文写信). More examples:

我们可以用学校食堂来开舞会。We can use the school cafeteria to hold the dance party.
你不应该用上班的时间来做自己的事。You should not use office time to do your own business.

iv. "无所不能" ("there are no things that [sb./sth.] cannot do".) 无所不V structure is again a double negative with a literary flavor (see note one above). This structure is typically used with a monosyllabic verb and is different from those detailed in note one, in that 无 is not followed by a related noun.
Examples:
他无所不知。（知=知道）There is nothing he doesn't know. (He knows everything.)
我跟他无所不谈。 We talk about everything.

v. 爱 in this usage suggests "tend to, apt to." It can be used in expressions with a negative flavor, like: 他很爱生病。 It's easy for him to get sick . (He always gets sick.)
Some other examples:
这只狗不爱叫。This dog usually doesn't bark.
这里夏天爱下雨。 It rains often here in the summertime.

同意		tóngyì	V to agree (with)
另(外)		lìngwài	ADJ another, the other...
道理		dàolǐ	N reason, logic
有道理		yǒu dàolǐ	VP/ADJ (sth.) to make sense, be logical
部落		bùluò	N tribe
象征	象徵	xiàngzhēng	V/N to symbolize; symbol; symbolism
蛇		shé	N snake (M. tiáo 条)
鹿		lù	N deer (M. zhī 只)
鸟	鳥	niǎo	N bird (M. zhī 只)
当...以后	當...以後	dāng...yǐhòu	TW after
特点	特點	tèdiǎn	N characteristics
集中		jízhōng	V/N to concentrate; concentration
鹰	鷹	yīng	N eagle (M. zhī只)
爪		zhuǎ/zhǎo	N claw, paw
角		jiǎo	N horn (of an animal)
游		yóu	V to swim
缘故	緣故	yuángù	N reason, cause
由于	由於	yóuyú	CONJ due to, because (of)
权力	權力	quánlì	N (authority) power
朝代		cháodài	N dynasty
夏朝		Xià cháo	N Xia Dynasty (ca. 21-16 century B.C.)
皇帝		huángdì	N emperor
子孙	子孫	zǐsūn	N offspring
望子成龙	望子成龍	wàng zǐ chéng lóng	PH to hope one's child will amount to something
成为	成爲	chéngwéi	EV (after a time) to become (sb./sth.)
成语	成語	chéngyǔ	N (usu.) four-character idiom; set phrase
西方		xīfāng	PW the West
题目	題目	tímù	N title, topic

回答问题：

1.为什么大为对龙的印象最深？
2.为什么王老师说龙的问题很复杂？
3.为什么有人说龙跟闪电有关？为什么有人说龙跟动物有关？
4.龙的形象有什么特点？这些特点是怎么来的？
5.中国的皇帝为什么要把自己称作龙？
6.“望子成龙”是什么意思？

语言结构

Focusing on Structure

I. "不是……吗" "Búshì...ma" as a Rhetorical Question Form

"不是……吗" as in "西方不是也有龙的神话吗？" is used as a rhetorical question form, serving as a reminder or emphasis of a known fact or an assumption. The example sentence above means, "The West also has mythologies about dragons, doesn't it?" Note that 不是 for this usage does not receive stress in speech, but the fact or assumption --the words following 不是 -- does receives stress. Compare these two sentences, whose meanings are differentiated by stressing different elements:

他<u>不是</u>中国人吗？ **Isn't** he Chinese? (The speaker did not know that he is no Chinese.)

他不是<u>中国人</u>吗？ He is **Chinese,** isn't he?/Isn't it the case that he is Chinese?

(The speaker thinks/assumes that he is Chinese)

The rhetorical usage of 不是……吗 can be used either to show the speaker's surprise at a situation opposite to his/her expectation based on his/her assumption, or to remind the listener of a fact. Here are some more examples:

你不是<u>已经走了</u>吗？怎么又回来了？

你不是<u>不喜欢牛奶</u>吗？怎么还买呢？

你不是<u>有个朋友在那个公司</u>吗？我们可以找他帮忙。

II. Using "Verb +作"

作 is often attached to a verb to mean "as" (e.g. to [address, regard, use, etc] somebody or something as...). It is often used with 把 when the topic is a person. Words such as 用、看、称、叫、当、比，etc. are commonly used with 作. Examples:

从前中国人常把皇帝称作龙。	In the past Chinese people often addressed emperors (with the term) "dragon."
我把她看作我的姐姐。	I regard her as my big sister. (Incorrect: 我看她我的姐姐。)
中国人常常把自己比作龙的子孙。	Chinese often liken themselves to the descendants of the dragon.
你可以把桌子当作床（来睡）。	You can treat the table as a bed to sleep on.
我们可以把这间屋子用作办公室。	We can use this room as an office.

词汇用法
Word Usage

Verbs

- 参观：参观一个地方(博物馆、学校...)；参观过几次；参观了三天；应邀到美国来参观
- 崇拜：崇拜一个人(神、龙...)；你最崇拜谁？/我对他很崇拜。
- 理解：他很理解我(我的想法\做法\感情\态度...)。/我不理解他为什么这么做。/我需要你的理解(N)。
- 出现：书架上出现了很多新书。/他是什么时候出现的？/出现过几次；他的出现使晚会更热闹了(N)。
- 同意：我很同意他的看法。/我不同意你的说法(你这样做)。
- 游：在水里游；游来游去；游得很快；从这里游到那里。
- 讨论：讨论事情(问题...)；跟同学讨论了好几次；讨论完了；我喜欢上讨论课(Mod)。
- 统一：统一国家(看法、考试...)；他们把几个小国统一起来。/这两个国家已经统一了。/对这件事，我们没有统一的看法。/我们的看法不统一(Adj)。
- 成为：他会成为一个很有能力的人。/他们没有成为朋友。/这件事成为了一个很麻烦的问题。

Adjectives

- 复杂：这个问题(那件事、情况...)很复杂。/他的性格很复杂。/做这件事很复杂。
- 深：水很深；颜色很深；印象很深；道理太深，很难懂。/他给我一个很深的印象。

Nouns

- 印象：印象很深；我对那个人(地方...)印象很好。/我对那个地方(那个人、那件事、那个东西...)没什么印象。/那个地方（留）给我一个很深的印象。
- 道理：道理很简单(复杂)。/你懂不懂这个道理？/你的说法有道理(没有道理)。
- 象征：部落(朝代、权力、喜事...)的象征；红色象征喜事(V)。
- 权力：龙象征最高权力；他有很大的权力。/他很有权力(Adj)。
- 题目：考试(作文、讨论...)的题目；今天要讨论的题目不多。

句型和习惯用语

Sentence Patterns and Expressions

1. (.......)不是......吗？**(Rhetorical: Isn't it the case that...?)**

- 西方不是也有龙的神话吗？ The West also has myths about dragons, doesn't it?
- 你不是跟他吹了吗？怎么现在又好起来了？
- 你不是说____________________________________吗？
- You know that scholar very well, don't you? Then let's invite him to our seminar (讨论会).

2. 无所不(monosyllabic verb) **(There is nothing that sb.\sth...does not V)**

- 我跟她无所不谈。
  There is nothing that she and I cannot talk about. (We talk about everything.)
- 他很有学问，可以说他无所不知。
- 中国古代，很多人认为龙____________________________
- She has been working here for more than twenty years. So there's nothing she can't do in this office.

3. 无(monosyllabic noun)不(monosyllabic verb) **(There is no...that sb.\sth. not V...)**

- 这个人无事不做。There is nothing this man doesn't do. (He does all kinds of things.)
- 她结婚的事无人不知。 Everyone knows about her getting married.
- 这个学者太喜欢看书了，可以说他________________________
- There is nothing I can't talk with my parents about.

4. 据...所Verb，...**(According to....../based on what is said, reported, etc. [from source])**

- 据我所知，他是学经济的。 As far as I know, he is an economics major.
- 据报上所说，今年的庆祝活动特别热闹。

- 据书上所说，______________________________
- According to what he said, many scholars have conducted research on dragon mythology.

5. A跟B很相似 **(A and B are very much alike / A is similar to B)**

- 龙的形象跟闪电很相似。The shape of the dragon is similar to that of lightning.
- 他的性情跟你的很不相似。His temperament is very different from yours.
- 我觉得 ______________跟 ______________________
- His ideas are similar to that scholar's.

6. ....，这就是...的缘故 **(..., and that is the reason why...)**

- 他昨天病了，这就是他(为什么)没有来的缘故。
  He was sick yesterday. That's why he didn't come.
- 她不但聪明能干，而且也很体贴人，这就是她(为什么)那么受欢迎的缘故。
- 小孩子给长辈拜年的时候，长辈按习惯要给小孩子红包，______________
- The color red symbolizes happy events. That's why it is the main color for holiday decorations.

7. 用......来.....**(... use sth. to do sth. /serve the purpose of...)**

- 很多部落都用动物来做部落的象征。
  Many tribes used animal images to serve as their tribal emblems.
- 中国人用放鞭炮来庆祝新年的到来。.
- 他寂寞的时候，常常用 ____________________来使自己高兴起来。
- I want to master Chinese to use it to help me in my future research.

文化介绍

Learning About Culture

十二生肖

The Twelve Animals of the Chinese Zodiac: The Dragon and Others

The Dragon is one of twelve animals (Rat, Ox, Tiger, Hare, Dragon, Snake, Horse, Sheep/Ram, Monkey, Rooster, Dog, and Pig) associated with the twelve "earthly branches," one part of a centuries-old system of recording time. (The other 'part' is called the ten "heavenly stems," jiǎ 甲, yǐ 乙, bǐng 丙, dīng 丁, etc.) By the second century A.D., the twelve "earthly branches" had become associated with the twelve animals in a rather complicated horoscope system.

Later, each hour of the day, each day of the year, and past and future years were all associated with the "stems" and "branches" and the animals as well. The particular combination of all these in effect at the moment of one's birth (i.e. one's 'sign'), when also linked to the Five Elements (see Lesson 7), was believed to have an effect on a person's luck or lack of it. Chinese even believed that they are born with the qualities of the animal that was associated with the year in which they were born. So if you were born in the Year of the Rat, you are held to be smart, cunning, brave and clever. The Horse Year child is expected to have stamina, the Snake to exhibit wisdom, the Ram to show good judgement in business, etc. The entire year, also associated with a particular animal, took on the coloration of the particular animal. Many Chinese still believe, for example, that the year of the Rat will be a year of bumper crops while the year of the Dragon, due to the power of a Dragon, is an especially auspicious year. Chinese "believe" that a "dragon son", i.e. a son born in the Year of the Dragon, will surely be intelligent and full of ability. Such a son will go far in his career.

These beliefs affected the arrangement of marriages. There are still families even today who compare the horoscopes (the "signs"!) of the prospective bride and groom. An age-old, often consulted book, called the Family Almanac, based upon the twelve-year animal cycle, tells us that: a "Horse-year person" dreads the "Ox"; that the Sheep and the Rat can live together for a while but will surely part; the Snake and Tiger are mortal enemies; the Hare and the Dragon will meet with sorrow if wed, and the Pig and the Monkey will never see happiness. But, it also predicts that the Rat and Ox, Tiger and Pig, Dragon and Rooster, Snake and Monkey, Horse and Sheep, Hare and Dog are pairs with promising futures. So when you choose a mate, know your own "sign" and that of your prospective spouse! Just ask 你属什么? (nǐ shǔ shénme?, "what's your sign?" When a Chinese talks about his/her sign, he/she will say “我属 (name of animal)”, not “我是...人!”

By the way, the Ten Heavenly Stems, in a more practical application, are in common use today serving much like our A, B. C, D, (甲乙丙丁) jiǎ, yǐ, bǐng, dīng, etc.) for listing series of things, like grades in Chinese schools!

你 属 什 么？

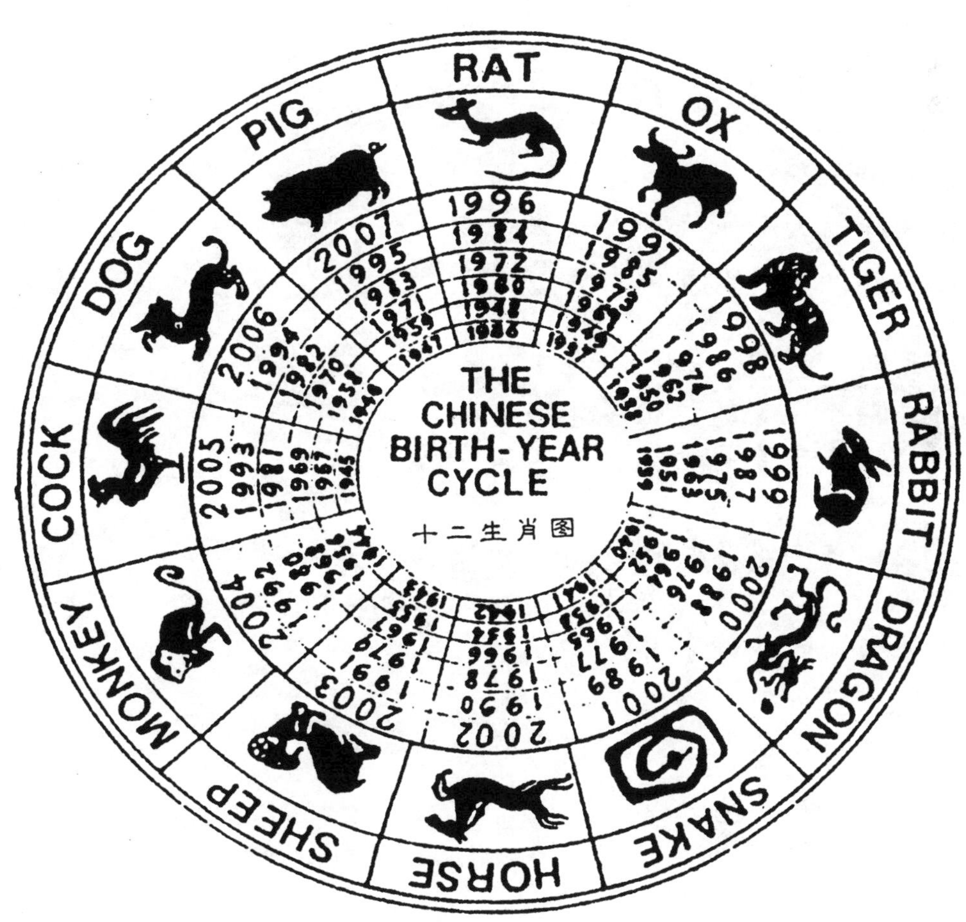

第十三课听力练习

第一部分：单句

请你们听下面的句子。每个句子的意思是什么？请在三个选择中选出一句来。

1. (a)他对中国文化不感兴趣。
   (b)他对中国文化不了解。
   (c)他对中国文化很有研究。

2. (a)我想象不出来他会做什么坏事。
   (b)他什么坏事都做，根本不是好人。
   (c)他是个好人，可是不爱做事。

3. (a)我听说那位老师对学生就象对自己的孩子一样。
   (b)我不清楚那位老师是怎么教学生的。
   (c)我听说那位老师不怎么照顾学生。

4. (a)这两个国家对老人的态度不一样。
   (b)这两个国家的文化差不多。
   (c)这两个国家的文化完全不同。

5. (a)他们俩有很多相似的地方，所以很谈得来。
   (b)他们俩很有趣，都喜欢谈经济方面的事。
   (c)他们俩讨论的事都很有趣。

6. (a)小李不喜欢那个人，觉得那个人跟狗差不多。
   (b)小李爱狗，觉得狗跟人一样聪明。
   (c)小李觉得那个人跟狗一样可爱。

第二部分：对话

第一遍:下面是小张和小王的对话。请听懂对话的大意，然后回答问题。

问题：小张和小王主要在谈些什么？

a)怎样找到一个轻松舒服的工作

b)小王公司的两位总经理

第二遍:请你们读下面的句子，然后把这个对话再听一次。听完后，看看这些句子说得对不对。

1. 小王对新总经理的印象不太好。
2. 新总经理很有学问，对工作上的事无所不知。
3. 新总经理不摆架子，他对人很客气。
4. 以前的总经理因为喜欢摆架子，所以不受人欢迎。
5. 新总经理和以前的总经理，做法和看法完全不一样。

第三遍:请你们读下面的问题，然后听第三遍。听完后，请回答问题。

1. 新总经理为什么很受公司里的人欢迎？

2. 以前的总经理为什么不受人欢迎？

3. 新总经理和以前的总经理在什么地方很相似？

第十三课 练习

词汇；句型；语法

I.填空：

参观：去年我________很多__________。/我们在_______参观_____三天。

印象：我______那个地方的印象很______。/她______我留下一个很________________________。

出现：今天早上桌子上出现了___________。/那个人昨天______________两次，今天又__________。/以前也曾经__________________这种现象。/他突然__________________我的面前。

同意：我很同意_______________。/我不同意把______________看作_________。/我非要跟他结婚不可，所以我父母只好______________。

相似：你的说法_____他的很相似。/_________________________有很多相似的地方(similarities, similar aspects)。

讨论：我们今天要讨论_______________________。/他们讨论_____三次，讨论_____________很好。/这个问题，你们什么时候能讨论____________?/这次的讨论很______________。

象征：龙象征__________。/白色象征_________。

道理：你说的话_____________。/这个道理___________，连小孩子都懂。

V-作：把________看作_________________；把_________比作___________________；　把_______称作________________

理解：我很理解______________。/他______我的___________很不理解。/我真不理解你为什么__________________。

据：据她______，这个字有两个意思。/据我_____，你们最好先去北京，再去上海。/据我所_______，他沒有去过中国。/据书上_____，________________。

II.改写下面的句子：

1.这个字的用法和那个字的差不多。（A和B很相似）

2.他的架子太大，所以我对他没有什么好感。（这就是.....的缘故）

3.这个人很有学问，他什么书都看，所以什么都知道。(无N不V；无所不V)

4.这本书上说，古代其实真的有龙这种动物。(据...所...)

5.他告诉我，美国人用鹰做象征可能是他们崇拜鹰的结果。（据.....;A和B有关）

6.从前人们在门上贴门神画，是为了把鬼赶跑。（用......来......）

III.用"V作"改写下面的句子：(看作、用作、比作、叫作、写作）

1.我很喜欢我们的公司，我觉得它好象就是我的家一样。

2.这本书上说，男人就好象太阳，女人就好象月亮。

3.据说这种飞机也可以当船用。

4.“国语”的另一个名字是“普通话”。

5.“龍”字的简体字是“龙”。

阅读练习

龙和凤

中国人一说到龙，就自然会想到凤1。凤是凤凰2的简称3，是中国古代神话中的一种神鸟4。据神话上说凤凰非常美丽5，身上长着五色的羽毛6，很像孔雀7，可是它的头又很像鸡8。据说凤凰一出现，天下9就会平安无事10。所以在古代，人们都希望看到凤凰，并把它看作吉祥11的象征。后来凤也就成了中国文化中一个和龙相对12的象徵:龙代表的是男性，凤代表的是女性，所以皇帝把自己称作龙，皇后13把自己称作凤。龙代表能力和权力，而凤代表美丽和高贵14。中国人也因此15把龙凤看作幸福16美满17的象征。有句老话18说："生儿愿成龙，生女愿成凤19"， 就是这个缘故。

在中国人的日常生活20中，龙和凤的形象常常同时21出现。有一个有名的广东22菜就叫作"龙凤配"；其实菜里既没有龙也没有凤，而只是蛇和鸡。贺年卡23上常常会印着24一对龙和凤，写着"龙凤呈祥"四个字，意思是祝人们在新的一年里美满。不少人按照传统风俗习惯订婚25结婚时，礼物26上或装饰品上也常有龙凤的形象。另外，中国人也爱用龙和凤这两个字给孩子起名27:男孩子叫龙，女孩子叫凤。如张家有两男两女，男的叫作大龙、小龙，或者大龙、二龙；女的叫作大凤、小凤，或者三凤、四凤。

现在虽然龙凤的形象还常常出现在装饰物上，但是人们多半把它看作象征幸福美满的传统艺术28，而不是权力、高贵的象征了。

生词表（查出或猜出空着的词语）：

1. 凤 [fèng] phoenix
2. 凤凰 [fènghuáng] phoenix
3. 简称 ______
4. 神鸟 ______
5. 美丽 ______
6. 羽毛 [yǔmáo] feather
7. 孔雀 [kǒngquè] peacock
8. 鸡 [jī] rooster, chicken
9. 天下 ______
10. 平安无事 to have peace
11. 吉祥 [jíxiáng] favorable auspices
12. 相对 ______
13. 皇后 [huánghòu] emperess
14. 高贵 ______
15. 因此 ______
16. 幸福 [xìngfú] happy; happiness
17. 美满 (of family) perfect, full
18. 老话 ______
19. 生儿愿成龙...... ______
20. 日常生活 ______
21. 同时 ______
22. 广东 ______
23. 贺年卡 New Year's cards
24. 印着 imprinted
25. 订婚 [dìnghūn] be engaged in marriage
26. 礼物 ______
27. 起名 ______
28. 艺术 [yìshù] art, craft

回答问题：下面哪一句对？

1. a.凤凰是古代的一种鸟，长得很像孔雀和鸡。
   b.凤凰是中国神话里的一种鸟，样子和孔雀很相似。

2. a.据说，古代的人都希望看见凤凰，因为它的出现会带来吉祥。
   b.因为凤凰长得非常美丽，而且是神鸟，所以古代的人都想看见凤凰。

3. a.后来，凤成了跟龙相对的象征，代表最高权力。
   b.中国皇后的象征是凤，因为凤代表美丽和高贵，和龙相对。

4. a.中国人爱把龙和凤放在一起，用来象征幸福美满。
   b.从前中国人希望自己的儿子能做皇帝，女儿能做皇后。

5. a.日常生活中人们用龙凤做装饰时，主要用它来代表男性的权力和女性的高贵。
   b.现在人们用龙凤做装饰时，不太重视"权力""高贵"的这个象征意义了。

口语练习

I.练习用"不是......吗"反问句回答：

（例子）　甲：我明年要到中国去。　乙：你不是刚从中国回来吗？怎么又要去了？

学生甲	学生乙
1.我的朋友要给我介绍一个对象。	________
2.昨天我去参观了中国历史博物馆。	________
3.他想在下课以后跟我们讨论一下西方的神话。	________
4.这件事很复杂，我不知道该找谁帮忙。	________
5.哎呀，我把他的地址忘了，现在怎么到他家去？	________

II. 练习下面的动物名称:

1. 大象 [dàxiàng]	5. 猴子 [hóuzi]	9. 狐狸 [húli]	13. 狼 [láng]
2. 老虎 [lǎohǔ]	6. 老鼠 [lǎoshǔ]	10. 猫 [māo]	14. 牛 [niú]
3. 狮子 [shīzi]	7. 兔子 [tùzi]	11. 乌龟 [wūguī]	15. 犀牛 [xīniú]
4. 熊 [xióng]	8. 熊猫 [xióngmāo]	12. 羊 [yáng]	16. 猪 [zhū]

据中国传统的说法，你属(shǔ)什么？有什么特点？

III. 谈动物特点及象征意义

中国文化中很多动物都有象征意义。比如说：狐狸、老鼠、狮子、羊、兔子、猴子、牛、狗，乌龟等等（请问一下你的中文老师这些动物都象征什么）。你的文化里哪些动物有象征意义？它们代表的是好的形象还是不好的形象？

写作练习

<u>谈动物</u>：

1. 请你谈一下你的文化里有没有龙或者跟龙相似的神话动物。它是什么样子？有什么能力和特点？有什么象征意义？跟中国文化中的龙有什么不同的地方？
2. 你最喜欢或者最不喜欢的动物是什么？请你说说它的形象、特点、生长在什么样的环境里，靠什么生活等等。为什么你（不）喜欢它？

“这个味道有点儿不对”

—做中国菜—

第十四课

Situation	Structure	Culture
语言情景	语言结构	文化介绍

In this lesson you join Hailin and Desheng as they cook up some Chinese food. Desheng is the willing teacher and Hailin the eager student of the art of Chinese cooking.

In terms of grammar you will focus on two usages of Verb+成 and also take a look at some other useful sentence patterns and expressions.

Culturally, in this lesson, the topic is the lore of Chinese food. So bring along your appetite!

"这个味道有点儿不对"

--做中国菜--

自从海琳和德生认识了以后，他们就成了朋友。德生是学化学的，别看他平常像个书呆子，其实他的兴趣很广。比如说，他对中国菜的做法和吃法就很内行。他说做中国菜有很多道理和学问。有的菜炒着[i]好吃，有的菜煮着好吃，凉性[ii]的菜吃多了容易胃疼或者泻肚，热性的吃多了容易上火，等等。另外，不同地方的人饮食的习惯也不一样：四川菜比较辣，而广东菜却比较温和，带点甜味；而且广东人爱在肉或者鸡里放点儿参什么的一起煮，这样更有营养。做得好的菜得色、香、味都有才行，也就是说，看着好看，闻着好闻，吃着好吃。海琳正想学做中国菜，于是就请德生教他。

德生：做菜以前你得先计划一下做些什么，应该有荤有素、有凉有热，这样对身体才好。

海琳：好了好了，你快教我怎么做吧。

德生：那你想学做什么菜？或者你喜欢吃什么？

海琳：我什么都想学，什么都喜欢吃。随你便吧，你说做什么我就学什么。

德生：好，我们来[iii]个三菜一汤怎么样？一个红烧鱼，一个炒豆腐，一个凉拌黄瓜，一个——什么汤呢？

海琳：酸辣汤！这是我最喜欢吃的。

---

i. "炒着好吃" ("[by means of] stir-frying [it's] tastier"--It tastes better stir-fried.) 着 used this way suggests "means."

Examples:

这件事说着容易做着难。	Talking about this is easy, but doing it is hard.
我要走着去学校。	I'll go to school on foot. (by means of walking)
坐着比站着舒服。	Sitting is more comfortable than standing.

ii. -性 ("-natured") is often affixed to an adjective to form an abstract noun.

Examples:

复杂	(complex)	复杂性 (complexity)	你看到这件事的复杂性没有？
重要	(important)	重要性 (importance)	这件事的重要性在哪里？
可能	(possible)	可能性 (possibility, feasibility)	做这件事有多大的可能性？

iii. "我们来个三菜一汤" ("Let's have a three-dish-and-one-soup [meal].") 来 is often used in ordering or planning meals.

Examples:

你想喝点什么？——（给我）来点茶吧。What would you like to drink? -- Let me have some tea.

小姐，请你给我们来两个酸辣汤。 Miss, we would like to have two orders of hot and sour soup.

味道		wèidao	N flavor, taste
化学	化學	huàxué	N/ADJ chemistry; chemical
平常		píngcháng	ADJ/MA normal, usual, ordinary; normally
比如说	比如說	bǐrú shuō	PH for example, for instance
内行		nèiháng	N/ADJ expert;skilled (ant.外行amateurish)
炒		chǎo	V to saute, stir-fry
煮		zhǔ	V to boil, cook in water
-性		-xìng	BF -natured, -ness, gender (used as N-Suf.)
凉性	涼性	liángxìng	N "cool-natured" (of food or Chinese medicine)
胃		wèi	N stomach
上火		shàng//huǒ	VO [Chin. med.] to suffer from too much internal heat (with symptoms such as constipation, or inflammation of the nasal and oral cavities)
饮食	飲食	yǐnshí	N diet
四川		Sìchuān	PW (name of a province in Southwest China)
比较	比較	bǐjiào	V/A to compare; comparatively,relatively
辣		là	ADJ (spicy) hot
而		ér	CONJ whereas, but, on the other hand
却		què	A but, however (used with 可是,而 etc.)
广东	廣東	Guǎngdōng	PW (name of a province in China)
温和	溫和	wēnhé	ADJ mild
参	參	shēn	N ginseng
营养	營養	yíngyǎng	N nutrition, nourishment
也就是说	也就是說	yě jiùshì shuō	PH that is to say, that means, in other words
香		xiāng	N/ADJ aroma,smell of cooked food; aromatic
闻	聞	wén	V to smell
计划	計劃	jìhuà	V/N to plan; plan, plot
荤	葷	hūn	N [lit] cooked food containing meat or fish
素		sù	N [lit] vegetarian food, vegetable food
随你便	隨你便	suí nǐ biàn	PH do whatever you like, do as you please
紅烧	紅燒	hóngshāo	VP to stew with soysauce
豆腐		dòufu	N beancurd, tofu
凉拌	涼拌	liángbàn	VP to make a cold dish by mixing vegetable and sauce
黄瓜	黃瓜	huángguā	N cucumber

德生：那好吧。我们现在就去买菜。

（一个小时后）

海琳：鱼炸好了，现在该放[iv]什么了？

德生：把鱼拿出来，锅里留点油，炒一下酱，再把鱼放进去。然后放上一点酒、酱油、糖、盐、葱、姜、蒜，还有这些作料，加一点水，让它煮一会儿。

海琳：......都放好了。

德生：现在我们来切黄瓜。......欸 (éi)，这个鱼的味道怎么有点儿不对？闻着酸酸的。

海琳：酸？我怎么没闻见？哎呀，真有酸味。糟了！一定是我把醋当作酱油了！那怎么办？

德生：我来尝尝。——哎呀，你真的放成醋了。我的天，好酸！

海琳：都怪我没看清楚！现在怎么办呢？

德生：别急别急，想个办法。这样吧，我们再加一点糖，就把它做成——

海琳：糖醋鱼！好主意好主意！来，我快放点儿糖进去。

德生：这回小心点儿啊，别又放成盐了。要是做成"盐醋鱼"——又咸又酸——哈哈，那就真的吃不成了！

iv. "放一点糖" ("put some sugar [into...]" is different from "加一点糖" ("add more sugar") . Normally 放 (not 加) is used for adding ingredients into food or other mixtures during the process of preparation. 加, on the other hand, implies adding an *additional* amount of an ingredient which is already included.
ration. 加, on the other hand, implies adding an *additional* amount of an ingredient which is already included.

酸		suān	ADJ sour
炸		zhá	V to deep-fry
锅	鍋	guō	N (Chinese) cooking pot, pan, "wok"
酱	醬	jiàng	N thick sauce made from soybeans and flour etc.
葱		cōng	N scallion
姜	薑	jiāng	N ginger
蒜		suàn	N garlic
作料		zuóliào	N side-ingredient, dressing (for cooking), seasoning
切		qiē	V to cut, slice
糟了		zāole	IE "Oh, darn it!"
醋		cù	N vinegar
当作	當作	dàngzuò	EV to treat sb./sth. as
酱油	醬油	jiàngyóu	N soy sauce
尝	嚐	cháng	V to taste, sample (food)
怎么办？	怎麼辦？	zěnme bàn?	PH "What should I (we) do now?"
急		jí	V/SV to panic, worry; worried, anxious
糖		táng	N sugar; candy
小心		xiǎoxīn	SV be careful
盐	鹽	yán	N salt

判断出以下词语的意思：

三菜一汤	三菜一湯
红烧鱼	紅燒魚
酸辣汤	酸辣湯
闻见	聞見
我的天！	
糖醋鱼	糖醋魚

回答问题：

1.德生说中国菜的做法和吃法有些什么道理？
2.请你说说四川菜和广东菜有什么不同。
3.“色、香、味”是什么意思？
4.按照德生的做法，红烧鱼应该怎么做？
5.为什么鱼的味道有点酸酸的？
6.他们原来计划做什么鱼？后来做成什么鱼了？

语言结构

Focusing on Structure

Two Usages of Verb-成: Transformation and Realization

成 can be attached to a verb introducing a resultative complement. There are two types of Verb-成 complements:

1. A Verb-成 B:

   成 in this usage denotes a sense of transformation from one thing to another ("become" "into"). Depending on the context, the transformation or change may be unintentional (e.g. a mistake) or intentional (e.g. done for a purpose). In either case, however, B indicates the final result. 把 is used in this structure if the agent of action is present and when the verb is transitive.

Examples:

Sb.把 A verb-成 B

- 我把糖放成盐了。I added salt instead of sugar (by mistake).
- 我常常把"你"字写成"他"字。I often write "ta" for "ni" (by mistake).
- 他想把这本书翻译(fānyì)成中文。He wants to translate this book into Chinese.

A verb-成 B:

- 生米已经做成了熟饭。The [raw] rice has been cooked.("What is done cannot be undone.")
- "你"字写成"他"字了。The word "ni" was miswritten as "ta".
- 那个小公司变成一个大公司了。That small company has now turned into a big one.

2. **Verb成 as a Resultative Compound:** 成 in this usage denotes "realization" of an action. It can be used for both actual or potential meanings.

Examples:

- 这件事我们做得成。We'll be able to do it [as we planned]. (This job can be done.)
- 我本来想去中国，可是没去成。I wanted to go to China, but it didn't work out.
- 昨天的晚会开成了吗？Was the party finally held last night?
- 我的电视机坏了，今天看不成电视了。My TV set is broken, so I can't watch TV today.

词汇用法
Word Usage

Verbs
- 炒：炒菜(饭、蛋、肉...)；菜炒得很好；把菜炒一炒；菜炒好了。
- 煮：煮饭(肉...)；饭煮熟(好)了；煮了一个多小时；还没煮好
- 尝：尝一尝菜(汤、肉...)的味道；你先尝一下。/你尝尝看。
- 炸：炸鸡(肉、鱼...)；把鱼炸一炸；炸得很好；把肉炸成金黄色
- 计划：计划出国留学(买房子、结婚的事...)；计划一下；计划得很好；做(定)计划(N)
- 闻：闻一闻是什么味？/我没闻见什么味。/我闻不出来这是什么味。

Adjectives
- 平常：很平常的人（事、东西、地方）；我平常不做饭。/平常他不说中文。(MA)
- 内行：对电脑很内行。/他在这方面很内行。/他是内行，可是我是外行。(N)
- 温和：性情(药性、天气...)很温和；他是个很温和的人。
- 酸：这个菜吃起来有一点酸；酸酸的；酸得不得了；这个菜是酸的。
- 辣：四川菜很辣；这个鱼是辣的。/辣辣的；辣得不得了；我不能吃辣的(东西...)。
- 香：这个菜闻着很香。/这种花不香。/这间屋子里有香味。/这个香味像花香(N)。

Nouns
- 营养：营养食品；牛奶的营养很高(很多)。/鸡蛋很有营养(Adj)。

Noun Suffixes
- -性：酸性；凉性；重要性；可能性；复杂性；男性/女性(male/female)

Others
- 比较：(V.)比较一下这两本书有什么不同。
  (N.)把这两本书做一个比较。
  (A.)他的中文比较好。/今天去比较方便。
- 随...便：去不去随你便。/今天去或者明天去都可以，随他便。

句型和习惯用语

Sentence Patterns and Expressions

1. 把AV成B... (take sth. for another; make sth. into another)

- 哎呀！你把酱油放成醋了！Oh no! You mistook vinegar for soy sauce! (You added vinegar instead of soy sauce.)
- 我刚才没注意，把"帅"字看成"师"字了。
- 他把"问"说成"吻"了，所以闹了个笑话。
- 你千万别把 ______________________
- The teacher didn't ask us to translate (翻译) the text into English.

2. V得成/V不成；V成了/没V成 (can\can't realize a plan; succeeded/failed in realizing/ fulfilling...)

- 我们最好早点儿买票，要不然可能就看不成那个电影了。We'd better buy the tickets early, otherwise we might not be able to see the movie.
- 我想买一套中式家具，可是没买成。
- 如果你把钱都用完了，那我们就______________________
- Several times he wanted to go to France, but he was never successful. This time he finally made it.

3. Verb着... (... by means of...; when done by way of...)

- 有的菜煮着好吃，有的菜炒着好吃。
  Some foods are tastier when stewed; others are tastier when stir-fried.
- 这个菜看着很漂亮，可是吃着没什么味道。
  This food looks beautiful, but it is tasteless.
- 这个房子看着______________，可是住着 ______________
- 你怎么总是______________________到学校去？
- This task looks complicated, but in fact it is quite simple when you do it.

4.别看......其实......(Don't be fooled/misled by [the fact that...] Actually......)

- 别看她很少念书，其实她的功课非常好。Don't be misled by her not studying much. Actually, she does very well on her school work.
- 别看他平常像个书呆子，其实他的兴趣很广。
- 别看他 ______________________________________,其实他很喜欢你。
- He looks as if he knows nothing, but don't be fooled. Actually, he knows everything.

5. .....,而 ....却..... ([clause], whereas/however ...)

que

- 四川菜比较辣，而广东菜却比较温和。
  Sichuanese cuisine tends to be spicy, whereas Cantonese cuisine is comparatively mild.
- 有的学者认为龙的形象跟自然现象有关，而有的学者却认为跟动物崇拜有关。
- 我父母要我毕业以后 __________________，而我却 ____________________
- Many scholars do not agree with him. However, I feel that his argument (说法) makes a lot of sense.

文化介绍

Learning About Culture

关于中国菜

About Chinese Food

There is much to consider when one talks about Chinese food because the Chinese enjoy cooking and eating. Here only a few aspects are briefly discussed.

When talking about cooking, almost everyone knows that regional differences exist. The particularities and specialties of each region are so vast that the subject merits a whole chapter by itself. In general, however, it is accepted by the Chinese that Cantonese food is light-tasting. Cantonese prefer fresh vegetables and sea food. Sichuan (Szechuan) food is highly spiced and peppery. Hunan produces many smoked foods. Northern food is more chunky and salty. Shanghai food is sweeter, and the people of Shanghai also like to use soy sauce.

Regardless of the regional particularities, there is a universal rule about Chinese cooking. Good Chinese cooking has to satisfy the three senses: sight, smell and taste. In preparing food, even colors should be in balance. Chinese food is distinguished according to five tastes: sour, sweet, bitter, hot (spicy) and salty. The five tastes should balance one another just like the colors of the food served. The smell of the food must be pleasant and stimulate the appetite.

Dietary taboos and supplements are another topic that concerns the Chinese. Although there are no hard and fast rules, folklore in every region has taught the Chinese what to eat and what not to eat. The idea, again, seems to be based on the sense of balance. Most foods, in these theoretical schemes, can be divided into two large categories, those which consist of elements that "heat" the body system, rè 热 "hot"; and those which "cool" it, liáng 凉 "cool" or hán 寒 "cold." To be healthy, one has to balance the hot and the cold. Green and bitter vegetables, for example, belong to the "cool" category. Fried food, being "hot" should be consumed only sparingly or with green vegetables. Finally, foods are body-building elements which replenish or rebuild one's health, according to certain characteristics. For example, chicken soup, beef soup or liver soup is believed to be a good and mild tonic for good health which one can enjoy all year around. For strong tonics, the Chinese cook their chicken or beef with certain herb medicines over low heat, simmering it for hours. This type of highly nourishing food, the Chinese believe, is better consumed in the cold winter, when the body system is at its weakest and nutrients can be readily absorbed. On the other hand, summer is not the time because the body system is normally more active.

Much more could be said about the food of China, but we hope that these few remarks have "whetted" your appetite!

第十四课听力练习

第一部分：单句

请你们听下面的句子。每个句子的意思是什么？请在三个选择中选出一句来。

1. (a)你为什么不会说“上”跟“下”这两个字呢？
(b)你为什么总是喜欢用“上”跟“下”这两个字呢？
(c)“上”、“下”这两个字，你为什么总是搞不清楚呢？

2. (a)做红烧鱼不能没有酱油。
(b)做红烧鱼哪里需要酱油！
(c)做红烧鱼有没有酱油都没关系。

3. (a)我今年一定去得成法国。
(b)我忙是忙，可是还有机会去法国。
(c)我今年大概没办法到法国去了。

4. (a)这把椅子又好看又舒服。
(b)这把椅子虽然不太好看，可是很舒服。
(c)这把椅子看起来很舒服。

5. (a)他是一个很有文化的人。
(b)他没有大学学历，可是学问很深。
(c)他只有学历，没有学问。

6. (a)他们两个长得不一样，但是很谈得来。
(b)他们两个长得差不多，也很有话说。
(c)他们两个喜欢讨论闪电的现象。

第二部分：对话

下面是小张和小王的几个对话。请你们把每个对话听两遍，然后回答问题。

1. 问：小王为什么不跟她的朋友去吃饭？
   (a)因为她是吃素的。
   (b)因为四川菜太辣，吃了以后她的胃会更不舒服。

2. 问：下面哪一句话是对的？
   (a)小李对做菜没有兴趣，所以常常上馆子吃饭。
   (b)小李虽然很少做菜，但是他其实做得很好。

3. 问：为什么小王用不同的方法做这两样菜？
   (a)因为这样做，这两种菜看着才比较漂亮。
   (b)因为这样做，这两种菜尝起来才都会好吃。

4. 问：小王为什么现在还没有电脑？
   (a)因为她没有钱，所以买不成电脑。
   (b)因为她的电脑被她姐姐借走了。

5. 问：下面哪一句话是对的？
   (a)小王去过好几次中国，今年还要再去一次。
   (b)小王从来没去过中国，今年大概能去成了。

6. 问：小王在红烧肉里放了什么？
   (a)醋
   (b)酱油

7. 问：下面哪一句话是对的？
   (a)小王把糖放成盐，所以他们吃不成糖醋鱼了。
   (b)小王相信她不会把糖放成盐。糖醋鱼一定作得成。

第十四课 练习

词汇；句型；语法

I. 选择适当的词语：

	a	b	c
1.他在电脑方面很________。	a.有道理	b.学问	c.内行
2.他知道这件事的________。	a.重要	b.重要性	c.很重要
3.身体好不好跟______习惯有关。	a.营养	b.饮食	c.计划
4.她是一个很______的人。	a.甜	b.凉性	c.温和
5.葱、姜、蒜都是做菜的______。	a.辣味	b.味道	c.作料
6.据说鸡______吃最有营养。	a.红烧	b.煮着	c.炸
7.我不吃肉，我是________。	a.吃素的	b.素	c.素食
8.我想让你________我做的菜。	a.试试	b.尝尝	c.吃了吃
9.这个菜的_____够了，可是不够_____。	a.盐/糖	b.咸/甜	c.糖/咸
10.他说______的菜吃了会_____。	a.热性/上火	b.凉性/上火	c.上火/热性
11.我昨天______晚饭做中国菜。	a.计划	b.做计划	c.计划了
12.据说四川菜多半是_____。	a.辣	b.热	c.辣的

II. 用"V-着"的适当形式填空：

1.你怎么老_______我？是不是我脸上有什么？

2.你别__________吃饭，这样对身体不好。

3.桌子上_________几本书，墙上_________一张画，门上______一张字条。

4.他现在还在门口__________，他已经站了半天了。

5.这种菜___________比__________好吃。

6.我们看完电影就______回学校去。________________，突然下起雨来了。

III. 用"-性"填空：

1.醋是_______________。/辣的东西是不是都是__________？

2.昨天来的人一半是___________。

3.我不知道做这件事有多大的______________。

4.这个问题其实不简单，可是他们都没看出这个问题的_______________。

IV.用“V成”的适当形式填空：(注意“-成”的不同意思和用法）

1.我忘了买鱼了，看样子今天晚上我们__________红烧鱼了。

2.我叫他做第十课的练习，可是他__________第十一课的了。

3.怎么搞的？我老把“他”字__________“你”字。

4.我本来准备今年学中文，可是这几个月来都忙得团团转，看样子又__________了。

5.我打算明年上研究所，可是现在还不知道______________。

6.你们两个人长得太像了，我每次都把你__________他。

阅读练习

谈“吃”

英文里有一句话说，“一个人吃着是肉，另一个人吃着是毒药1。”意思是说每个人的口味2不同，一个人喜欢吃的东西，另一个人可能就受不了。这句话一点不假3。我曾经在一个英国人家里住过一段时间。他们多半是把菜或者肉煮着吃，而且煮的时间很长，也不放什么作料，只是在吃的时候放点胡椒4和盐就行了。他们自己吃得津津有味5，而我们中国人吃着就觉得味道不够。

中国人最喜欢吃的、最常做的是炒菜。炒菜不但做起来快，而且吃起来也香。炒菜最常用的作料是葱、姜、蒜。锅热了以后，先把葱、姜、蒜，或者干辣椒6什么的放到油里炒一下，等香味出来了，再把主菜7下锅，放上盐、糖、酱油、等等。菜炒好后，可以放一点麻油8，这样菜吃着就会更香。

中国人以为中国菜好吃是作料放得多的缘故。可是印度人9吃中国菜时一定会说中国菜的味道不够，因为作料放得太少了！而且中国人的米饭里什么都不放，不好吃！有一次我去一个印度老师家做客，当饭菜放到桌上来的时候，我吃了一惊10：菜里饭里都花花绿绿11的，有各种各样的香料12、配料13。有的菜看着好看，闻着也蛮香，可是一尝，味道跟中药14差不多！可是他们认为这样做的饭菜味道才够，吃着才香。

除了菜的做法和吃法不同以外，不同文化的人吃食的习惯也不同。比如说，中国人吃饭时爱把碗放到嘴边去吃，而西方人多半是把碗和<u>盘子</u>15放在桌上。中国人常常最后喝汤，而很多别的国家的人是先喝汤再吃饭。中国人吃饭时也有很多规矩，而且有一些规矩跟迷信有关，这也是中国人和西方人不同的地方。

<u>查出下面的空着的词的意思</u>

1.毒药 [dúyào] poison	6.干辣椒 [gānlàjiāo] dried chili	11.花花绿绿 ___________
2.口味 ______________	7.主菜 ______________	12.香料 [xiāngliào] spices
3.假 [jiǎ] false, fake	8.麻油 [máyóu] sesame oil	13.配料 matching food or ingredients
4.胡椒 [hújiāo] pepper	9.印度人 ____________	14.中药 Chinese medicine
5.津津有味 ___________	10.吃了一惊 __________	15.盘子 [pánzi] plates

<u>据这篇短文的看法，下面说的什么地方不对？</u>

1.英国人认为肉是毒药。

2.英国人除了肉以外，什么都煮着吃。

3.英国人觉得他们做的菜没有什么味道。

4.中国人做菜放的作料最多，所以中国菜很香。

5.印度人觉得中国饭菜不够好吃，因为菜里的颜色不够，饭里的作料不够。

6.中国人认为作料放得多菜就好吃，所以中国人一定也很喜欢吃印度人做的菜。

7.中国人吃饭时候的规矩都跟迷信有关。

口语练习

I.<u>回答问题</u>：

1.中国菜里什么菜你不喜欢吃？为什么？

2.中国人的饮食习惯上有哪些跟你的习惯不一样？

3.你吃东西注意不注意营养？你认为营养重要吗？为什么？

4.如果需要减肥的话，你愿意节食（少吃东西）还是运动？

II.练习下面用"把"字结构的句子：

1.把___炸成金黄色　2.把_____打在碗里　3.把_____切成小块
4.把___用酱油拌一下　5.把_____炒出香味　6.把_____放进开水里煮三分钟

II.情景会话：

1.怎么做......？

有一个中国学生想学做三明治、蛋糕、和色拉（salad），请你教教他。（请用中文说。如果有的字你不会用中文说，那么你可以用简单的中文说出意思。）

2.到餐馆吃饭点什么菜？

你跟朋友到中国餐馆去吃晚饭。你想点什么菜？怎么点？（请表演一下，并从下面的菜单里选菜。）

蔬菜名称

白菜[báicài] Chinese cabbage　芥兰[jièlán] broccoli　胡萝卜[húluóbo] carrots
菠菜[bōcài] spinach　青椒[qīngjiāo] green pepper　茄子[qiézi] eggplant
四季豆[sìjìdòu] string beans　青豆[qīngdòu] fresh soybeans　雪豆[xuědòu] snow peas
豌豆[wāndòu] peas　豆芽[dòuyá] bean sprouts　蘑菇[mógu] mushroom

肉类/禽类	切法	做法
猪肉[zhūròu] pork	-片[-piàn] sliced...	鱼香[yúxiāng] cooked with garlic sauce
牛肉[niúròu] beef	-丁[-dīng] diced...	宫保[gōngbǎo] stir-fried (meat) (spicy)
羊肉[yángròu] lamb	-丝[-sī] shredded...	清炒[qīngchǎo] stir-fried w/o brown sauce
鸡[jī] chicken	-末[-mò] ground...	酸辣[suānlà] hot and sour
鸭[yā] duck	-丸[wán] -ball	糖醋[tángcù] sweet and sour

午餐 **LUNCH SPECIAL** 午餐

Mon. - Sun. 11:30am - 4:00pm
Served with Soup, Mixed Green Salad and Vegetable Fried Rice

Choice of Entrees

左宗棠鸡	General Tso's Chicken	7.00
芥兰鸡片	Chicken w. Broccoli	7.00
鱼香鸡	Chicken w. Garlic Sauce	7.00
什菜鸡	Chicken w. Mixed Vegetable	7.00
宫保鸡	Diced Chicken w. Peanuts	7.00
腰果鸡	Diced Chicken w. Cashew Nuts	7.00
素什锦	Saute Mixed Vegetables	6.00
麻婆豆腐	Ma Po Bean Curd	6.00
家常豆腐	Bean Curd Home Style	6.00
鱼香四季豆	String Beans w. Hot Garlic Sauce	6.00
鱼香芥兰	Broccoli w. Hot Garlic Sauce	6.00
清炒草菇芥兰	Saute Straw Mushroom w. Broccoli	6.00
鱼香肉丝	Shredded Pork w. Hot Garlic Sauce	5.50
回锅肉	Twice Cooked Pork	5.50
白菜叉烧	Roast Pork w. Chinese Bok-hoy	5.50
甜酸肉或鸡	Sweet & Sour Pork or Chicken	5.50
芥兰牛	Beef w. Broccoli	6.50
青椒牛	Pepper Steak	6.50
什菜牛	Beef w. Mixed Vegetables	6.50
干烧牛肉丝	Shredded Beef w. Hot Spicy Sauce	6.50
虾龙糊	Shrimp w. Lobster Sauce	7.50
干烧虾仁	Baby Shrimp w. Hot Spicy Sauce	7.50
宫保虾仁	Baby Shrimp w. Peanuts	7.50
腰果虾仁	Baby Shrimp w. Cashews	7.50
鱼香虾仁	Baby Shrimp w. Garlic Sauce	7.50
豆腐虾仁	Baby Shrimp w. Bean Curd	7.50
爆双丁	Baby Shrimp & Diced Chicken	7.50
葱爆三样	Baby Shrimp, Chicken & Pork w. Scallions	7.50
干炒牛河粉	Beef Chow Fen	5.00
咖喱鸡丝捞面	Chicken Lo Mein in Curry Sauce	5.00
咖喱鸡	Curry Chicken	5.00
咖喱海鲜炒饭	Seafood Curry Fried Rice	5.00
炒米粉	Rice Noodles (Chicken, Beef, or Veg.)	5.00

午餐 午餐

写作练习

1.介绍饮食习惯

很多中国人想了解西餐的吃法，如怎么点菜、先吃什么后吃什么、吃西餐时有什么餐桌规矩等等。请你介绍一下。（你也可以介绍其他文化的饮食习惯。）

2.怎么做......？

如果你会做菜或者做某种食品（三明治、汉堡包、蛋糕、色拉、等等，或者中国菜），请你介绍一种做起来简单方便而且好吃的食品。（把做的方法一步一步地写出来。）

练习用下面的句子：

先把......洗干净，切成.......；然后把.......，在......里放上......，再放上一点......。等......了以后，就可以把........。最后......，这样，.......就做好了。

校园生活一角

—布告栏—

第十五课

Situation	Structure	Culture
语言情景	语言结构	文化介绍

Here in Lesson 15 you meet Dawei in Beijing where he has discovered another way of learning about the culture and language of modern China. It's something we're all very familiar with in our own culture: public signs, notices, announcements and the sort of language that is common on such things. That kind of language, especially in Chinese, is characterized by a terseness, a formality, and a sort of literary flavor, not characteristic of the colloquial style. You'll be introduced to this feature of modern Chinese in this lesson.

In both our Structural and Cultural focus, you will learn about additional features of this so-called literary style or 书面语 (shūmiànyǔ).

校园生活一角

--布告栏--

在学校里大为发现了一个学中文的好地方，那就是学校餐厅旁边的布告栏。那里贴着各种各样的广告、启事、通知等等，从中[i]既可以学到很多词汇和用法，又可以了解到大学生们在想些什么、做些什么。所以每天大为都要到这里来看几分钟，今天他看到一些什么呢？

角		jiǎo	N corner
栏	欄	lán	BF (bulletin, newspaper) column, section
布告栏	佈告欄	bùgàolán	N bulletin board
餐厅	餐廳	cāntīng	N cafeteria; restaurant
启事	啓事	qǐshì	N a notice, written announcement (to public)
通知		tōngzhī	V/N to notify; notification, notice (to specific group or person)
既...又...		jì...yòu...	A both... and ...
词汇	詞彙	cíhuì	N vocabulary, terminology

i. .....,从中既可以...... (..., from which [one] can ...). 从中 is a shortened form of 从.....中 and is often used in formal style.

计算机初级班招生

好消息：我系将于七月中[ii]开办一期电子计算机初级班，学期为一周（共40学时）。欢迎我校师生报名参加学习。

学费：100元

报名时间：五月一日--七月一日

地点：计算机系一楼办公室

舞会通知

学生会将于本星期六晚八时至十二时在学校餐厅举行化装舞会，欢迎参加。

会	會	huì	N party, conference; committee
举行	舉行	jǔxíng	V [formal] to hold (party, meeting, etc.)
化装	化裝	huàzhuāng	V to disguise
计算机	計算機	jìsuànjī	N computer (PRC usage)
初级	初級	chūjí	N beginner level
招生		zhāo//shēng	VO to enroll new students
消息		xiāoxi	N news (as in "good news")
开办	開辦	kāibàn	V to start or set up [a school, business, etc.]
期		qī	M (school,course, etc.) term
学期	學期	xuéqī	N semester, term, duration (of a course, etc.)
报名	報名	bào//míng	VO to apply, sign up

ii. "七月中" here means "mid-July." 中 is used to mean "mid-" or "middle of" especially when it is attached to the name of a month/year or a monosyllabic term indicating a time frame, such as 月, 年 or 期. However, 中 ("midst") also suggests "during" or "in" or "within" in other cases. For example, 讨论中 (during/in the discussion), 在两年中 (within two years), or 在这两年中 (within/during these two years).

征友启事

我[iii]友，女，22岁，温柔可爱，欲找有责任心及事业心，并身高1.75米以上，年龄29岁以下的博士生为[iv]友。有意者请留电话或地址，或与3045513刘红联络。

您想找家教吗？

也许您正为自己或者子女考不上大学而着急？也许您已考进大学但又觉得功课太吃力？别着急：我们可为您提供补习各门功课的家教及课外辅导。时间灵活，价格合理，包您满意！请电2151309王。

征	徵	zhēng	V [formal] to solicit publicly, to seek
温柔		wēnróu	ADJ (person) gentle, tender
-心		-xīn	SUF -minded, [have] a conscience of
责任	責任	zérèn	N responsibility, duty
年龄	年齡	niánlíng	N age (of a person)
博士		bóshì	N (academic) doctor; Ph.D.
有意		yǒuyì	V/ADJ have interest; interested
家教		jiājiào	N private tutor
考上		kǎoshang	RV to pass (the entrance exam)
子女		zǐnǚ	N children ("sons and daughters")
吃力		chīlì	V/ADJ to consume strenuous effort; effort-taking
提供		tígōng	V supply, provide
补习	補習	bǔxí	V/N to take lessons in order to meet requirements; to give tutoring lessons
辅导	輔導	fǔdǎo	V/N to tutor, guide; tutoring (giving guidance)
灵活	靈活	línghuó	ADJ flexible, agile
价格	價格	jiàgé	N price
合理		hélǐ	ADJ reasonable, fair
包		bāo	V [colloq.] to guarantee (sb. for sth.)

iii. In the formal style "我" is used when the speaker refers to another party or speaks on behalf of another party. Note the different implications and translations in the following formal usages:
我友（=我的朋友） "my friend" (The speaker from a personal perspective)
我校（=我们学校） "our school" (The speaker speaking on behalf of the school or to a public audience)
我国（=我们国家） "our country" (The speaker speaking on behalf of the country or to a public audience)
In colloquial usage, however,"我的..." and "我们..." convey different messages. The speaker does not necessarily speak on behalf of the party referred to. For example:
我的学校很大。(我的 suggests ownership: The school I own is big.)
我们（的）学校很大。(我们学校 refers to the school with which the speaker is affiliated.)

iv. "为" here means "as", corresponding to 作 (as in 称作, 看作, etc.) in everyday usage. This is also why 为 can sometimes replace 作 in V-作 phrases, such as, 称为, 比为.

Literary/Written-Style Words and Their Colloquial Equivalents (based on usages in this lesson):

本		běn	SP our [school,company, etc.] (=我们这个) current, this [week, month, etc.] (= 现在这个，这个) myself (本人=我)
将	將	jiāng	A will (=要)
于	於	yú	CV at, in, on, etc. (= 在 as in 我是在中国生的)
至		zhì	PREP to, till (=到)
为	為	wéi	EV to be, as (=是；-作)
欲	欲	yù	AV to want to, wish to (=想V,要V)
与	與	yǔ	CONJ/CV and; with (= 跟,和)
及		jí	CONJ and, as well as
-者		zhě	N -person (=的人)
周	週	zhōu	M/N week (=星期)
时	時	shí	N o'clock; hour （=点钟；小时）

Abbreviated Words in this lesson (selective):

共		（一共）
师生	師生	（老师和学生）
并	並	（并且）
或		（或者）
电	電	（打电话...）
王		（一个姓王的人）
已		（已经）
但		（但是）

回答问题：
1.为什么大为每天要到布告栏去看几分钟？
2.布告栏上贴着些什么？
3、“舞会通知”上说有什么舞会？什么时候举行？在哪里举行？
4.写“征友启事”的是男性还是女性？有些什么要求(requirements)？
5.计算机班是为什么人开的？什么时候开始上课？
6.家教启事上说为什么样的人补习或辅导？补习或辅导些什么？

语言结构

Focusing on Structure

书面语体特点简介

A Brief Introduction to Chinese Written/Literary Style

The language conventionally used in journalism, advertising, and on public notices and signs, etc. is characterized by a literary flavor, a terseness and ellipsis (omission of words) not seen in the colloquial language. Such language is usually referred to as 书面语 in Chinese. In such language, many disyllabic words used in spoken Chinese are converted to monosyllables. For example, 但 for 但是, 可 for 可以, 已 for 已经, 且 for 而且, etc. Some spoken words have their literary counterparts. Here are some common ones: 为 for 是, 此 for 这个, 于 for 在, and 与 for 跟. Therefore, when the style switches from spoken to literary, the writer is expected to be consistent in choosing the appropriate words to match the style.

Examples:

书面语	口语
1.我将于明日离美。	=我（要）明天离开美国。
2.有意者请电2113087王。	=有兴趣的人，请打电话到2113087找一个姓王的。
3.我店将于本月开始销售新到电脑。	=我们商店这个月开始卖新到的电脑。
4.本系将于下月举行中国问题讨论会，欲参加者与系办公室联络。	=我们系下个月有一个中国问题的讨论会，想参加的人跟系办公室联络。

If one attempts to convert written or literary forms to spoken usage, difficulties often occur if one merely matches words according to meaning. One needs rather to add words necessary to make sentences consistent in style and grammar. The following are examples of wrong or incomplete conversion from the above examples of written/literary style.

⇒ (for No. 2 above) *有兴趣人请打电话2113087王。 (See above for appropriate conversion.)

⇒ (for No. 3 above) *他明天早五点时离开美。 (See above for appropriate conversion.)

词汇用法

Word Usage

Verbs

- 举行：举行活动(舞会、庆祝会...)；在北京举行；举行过两次
- 开办：开办一个班（学校、公司、补习班）；开办了两个月
- 报名：向（跟）老师报名；报名参加那个班；报过两次名
- 提供：提供机会(情况、设备、学习环境、住房)；他为我们提供了很多工作机会(很好的学习环境)。
- 补习：我要补习英语（数学、化学）。/他给（为）我补习过几次。/补习了半年；这半年的补习(N)很有帮助；补习学校；补习班(Mod)
- 辅导：他辅导我学英语。/他为我辅导化学。/辅导过几次；辅导了三天；他辅导得很好。/课外辅导(N)；他是我的辅导老师(Mod)。

Resultative Verb Compounds

- 考上：考上大学(研究所\院)；他去年没考上北京大学，今年可能考得上了。

Adjectives

- 温柔：性情(声音)很温柔；说话很温柔；她对你很温柔。
- 吃力：学习(工作、这门课)很吃力；我手上拿的东西太多，走起路来很吃力。
- 灵活：(时间、做事、动作...)很灵活
- 合理：价格(要求、做法、理由...)合理；合理的要求；这样做不合理。

Nouns; Noun Suffixes

- 角：桌子有四个角；街角；屋角
- 词汇：有用的词汇；口语〔的〕词汇；电脑方面的词汇；这本书的词汇很多。
- 会：晚会；聚会；舞会；今天我有两个会(meetings)。/学生会(committee)
- 启事：征友(结婚、招生...)启事；贴一张启事；启事上写着一些什么？
- 通知：(舞会、入学、开会...)通知；还没收到通知；公司通知我去面试(V)。
- 消息：我有一个好消息要告诉你。/你最近有他的消息吗？
- 年龄：他有多大年龄？/他的年龄大不大？/年龄在二十一岁以下的人不能喝酒吗？

- -心：事业心；责任心；爱心；自信心；他的事业心很强。/他很有事业心(ambitious)。

Others

- 初\初-：七月初；年初；九七年初；初级汉语；我初学汉语。
- 中\中-：七月中；年中；九七年中期；期中考试；中级英语
- 以上\以下：三十人以上；五十岁以下；38度以上；100元以下；大学以上水平

Literary/Written Style Words

- 本：本月（周、周末、学期、年）；本系（校、国）；本人(I,me)
- 与：我与他的关系；本学期与下学期；龙与闪电有关吗？/请你与他联络。
- 于：于本月五日开始上课；他于一九七五年生于中国北京。
- 欲：欲找女友；欲学电脑；欲移民美国；欲找进出口方面的工作；欲早日结婚
- 为：学期为一周；这个班里一半学生为女性（美国人）。/欲找一位研究 生为友
- 至：三点至五点；七月中至八月底；北京至上海
- 及：有事业心及责任心；老师、学生及其他人；学中文、化学及经济学
- -者：有意者；欲学电脑者；参加学习者；参观者；征友者；初学者

句型和习惯用语

Sentence Patterns and Expressions

1.从……中（看出来，了解到，发现，…）**(From ... [sb.] discover\learn about\ find, etc.)**

- 从学校布告栏的启事中可以了解到学生们在想些什么，做些什么。
  You can learn about what students are thinking and doing from the notices on the school bulletin board.
- 从他的谈话中，我听出来他是个很有学问的人。
- ______________________________，我学到了很多东西。
- From discussions with my classmates, I have learned a lot that I can't learn from books.

2. ……,从中V….**(..., from which, sb. [know,discover,etc.]....)**

- 我常常看中文报纸，从中可以了解很多中国的情况。
  I often read Chinese newspapers, from which I can learn about things in China.
- 他问了我很多学生生活方面的问题，从中我看出他对学生很关心。
- 他总是在图书馆里看书，______________________________
- Chinese scholars differ in their views regarding the dragon mythology. From this one can tell that the dragon mythology is a complex issue.

3. …既…又… **(...both... and ...)** 既不（没）…又不（没）…**(neither...nor...)**

- 他既有能力又有经验。
  He is both capable and experienced. (He has both ability and experience.)
- 他既不能吃辣的又不能吃酸的，那我只好给他做甜的吃了。
- 我的女朋友既______________又______________，所以我__________。
- I'd like to recommend this food to you ; it's both delicious and nutritious.

4. ……将于……V**(Sb. will do...\Sth. will be done [at time\place])**

- 我校将于下个月开始招生。
- 学生会将于本星期六晚在本校餐厅举行舞会。
- 这个公司将于______________开始在我校______________。
- 我将于 ______________到中国 ______________。

文化介绍

Learning About Culture

中国商店名称及公共牌示的语言特点

Language Used in Chinese Store Names and Public Signs

The language style and choice of words used in Chinese store names and public signs are quite different from those of daily speech. In general, the style is characterized by terseness and elegance with an elliptical structure and non-personal perspective.

Store names are often selected from words which bear meanings related to the particular type of business or merchandise. The words are usually of formal usage, often with a literary flavor and reflecting good prospects for the business. For example, for a women's clothing store, 女装店 is the term to be used instead of 女人衣服店. Here 装 is a short form for 服装 (fúzhuāng: wear, attire) or 时装 (fashion), a formal and refined term for 衣服. To individualize the store name, one may add some words (usually not just a single character) in front which are directly or indirectly related to the type of business, such as 新兴女装 ("Xīnxīng Women's Wear), or 佳美食品 (Jiāměi Foodstore). 新兴 ("new","in fashion") is congruent with clothing business in meaning; and 佳美 ("excellent", "fine") is associated with the expressions 佳肴 (jiāyáo: "delicacies") and 美味 (měiwèi: "fine flavor").

Some store names also choose words or characters which do not necessarily represent the type of business but express auspicious meaning. For example, a store name like 鑫金 (xīnjīn) suggests the desire for wealth and prosperity, as the character 金 (jīn: "gold", "money") is reduplicated. An interesting phenomenon in recent years is the tendency to adopt foreign-sounding names for stores or products, such as 蒙丽沙时装店 (Menglisha Fashion), 圣吉奥洗衣机 (Shengji'au Washing Machine). Although these names are not actually meaningful, they sound western to Chinese. The reason for this has to do with growing popularity of foreign products in China (i.e. Chinese consumers' growing interest in western products). In addition, although it is uncommon for Chinese to use real personal names for stores or products, names of celebreties have been appearing in some product, such as, clothing or cosmetics since the late 1980's. Moreover, for artistic or esthetic purposes, the traditional form of characters are often preferred for the store signs in China.

While store names show more consideration for auspicious meaning and fancy words, Chinese public signs tend to be formal, elliptical, direct and impersonal. Words are mostly abbreviated into monosyllables for brevity and economy of space. For example, 处 (chù) is used for 地方, 内 (nèi) for 里面, 售 (shòu) for 卖, 勿 (wù) for 不要 or 别. The following are some examples of public signs or placards.

入口/出口
rùkǒu / chūkǒu
Entrance / Exit

售票处(售票處)
shòupiào chù
Ticket Window

自行车停放处(自行車停放處)
zìxíngchē tíngfàng chù
Bicycle Parking Lot

此处禁止停放车辆
(此處禁止停放車輛)
cǐ chù jìnzhǐ tíngfàng chēliàng
No Parking

此路不通
cǐ lù bù tōng
Dead End

巷内有公厕
xiàng nèi yǒu gōngcè
Public Toilet In Alley

中山公园由此去(中山公園由此去)
Zhōngshān gōngyuán yóu cǐ qù
To Zhongshan Park

请勿吸烟/禁止吸烟
(請勿吸煙/禁止吸煙)
qǐng wù xīyān/jìnzhǐ xīyān
No Smoking

第十五课听力练习

第一部分：单句

请你们听下面的句子。每个句子的意思是什么？请在三个选择中选出一句来。

1. (a)小张喜欢跟我谈电子计算机方面的事。
   (b)我听了小张的谈话后，知道他很懂电子计算机。
   (c)小张有兴趣开办一个电子计算机班。

2. (a)看报纸可以帮助我们了解每个国家的最新情况。
   (b)我们都很关心报上的新闻。
   (c)报纸不能提供我们最新的消息。

3. (a)他想跟他母亲学习做中国菜。
   (b)他因为常跟着母亲做菜，所以学会怎么把菜做好。
   (c)他在做菜方面完全是个外行。

4. (a)他工作起来很吃力。
   (b)他是个很有事业心的人。
   (c)他什么事都做得很好，这说明他很有能力。

5. (a)下星期他打算办一个舞会。
   (b)他对下星期的舞会一点也不关心。
   (c)为了下星期的舞会，他最近忙得不得了。

6. (a)因为系里研究生的需要，才有了这个高级中文班。
   (b)这个高级中文班是系里的研究生开办的。
   (c)系里的研究生计划开办一个高级中文班。

7. (a)我们公司去年举行了三次新年晚会。
   (b)我们公司新年期间要举行晚会。
   (c)有一家公司新年期间要举行晚会。

第二部分：短文

第一遍:请你们听懂这篇短文的大意，然后回答问题。

问题：这个人在布告栏上发现了什么？

a)一个电脑班的招生广告

b)一个舞会通知

第二遍:请你们读下面的句子，然后把这篇短文再听一次。听完后，看看这些句子说得对不对。

_____1.这个人是在电脑中心的布告栏上看到的招生广告。

_____2.这个电脑班是专门为计算机系的学生开的。

_____3.这个电脑班的学费不贵，上课地点也很方便。

_____4.这个人对电脑是门外汉。

_____5.这个电脑班的报名地点在学生餐厅。

第十五课 练习
词汇；句型；语法

I.填空:

1.举行：学校昨天________。/明天的会________举行？/今年我们举行________三次欢迎会。

2.通知：公司通知我________。/我等了一个月，还没________入学通知。/我昨天是用________通知他们的。

3.有...心：她很有________心，一边工作还一边念博士。/这个工作很重要，需要一个有________心的人来做。/他们想找一个有________心的人照顾小孩。

4.考/考上：他想________研究所，可是________两次都________。如果下一次再________，他就不再________。

5.补习：我的英文很差，需要________。/他正在________孩子补习功课。/我________几个月，总算考上了大学。

6.辅导：如果你觉得这门课吃力，可以找一个家教________。/昨天下课以后，老师又给我辅导________半个小时。/他常常给学生辅导________，他辅导得________。

7.年龄/岁：他的年龄________？/她有________？/你年龄还________，不懂这个道理。

8.期/学期：学校下个月要开一________初级电脑班。/今年我们开了三________英文补习班，每________两个月。/上个________我一共上了五门课。/我学了两个________的中文了。

9.词/词汇：这个________的意思我不懂。/“报名”这个________的意思跟“申请”有一点不一样。/这一课有很多有用的________。/你熟悉不熟悉经济学方面的________？

II. 选择适当的词:

	a.	b.	c.
1. 我校将_____明日举行欢迎会。	a. 与	b. 于	c. 欲
2. 欢迎会七时_____九时在一号楼举行。	a. 到	b. 往	c. 至
3. 龙___凤的形象无处不在。	a. 与	b. 将	c. 为
4. 她想找一个研究生________友。	a. 为	b. 作	c. 及
5. 我们为您提供家教_______课外辅导。	a. 于	b. 及	c. 将
6. ________友今年二十二岁，大学毕业。	a. 本	b. 我	c. 者
7. 李先生现_______北京大学中文系教授。	a. 作	b. 是	c. 为

III. 请把下面的短语和句子改写成口语：

今早____________　　前晚八时____________　　本月初______________

本人____________　　本地______________　　本课________________

我友____________　　我校________________　　下月底______________

离美____________　　到京____________　　多为华裔女性________

2. 本店将于明早九时至晚八时出售进口电视机。

3. 我友现为北大研究生，欲找一有事业心女子为友。有意者电8913098李新。

IV. 哪一个是哪一个？

1. Public Phone
2. No Smoking
3. Reception Desk
4. Luggage Office
5. Ticket Window
6. Men's Room
7. No Parking
8. Information
9. No Visitors Allowed
10. (Train) Waiting Room
11. To Forbidden City
12. Lounge
13. Entrance
14. Cashier
15. WC

售票处　　谢绝参观

参观故宫由此去　　公用电话

请勿吸烟　　此处禁止停放自行车

盥洗室　　男厕　　休息室

收款台　　询问处　　行李寄存处

候车室　　入口　　服务台

阅读练习

（一）大学生征友趣闻1

某2大学计算机3系的几个男生有一天贴出一个征友启事，上面是这样写的：

计算机系三班的男士4向您问好！
本班有最能干、最聪明、最体贴人的男士，
望与大方5、善良6女生为友。欢迎您应征7。
有意者请访8二号楼三零五室。

这个启事出了不久，有一个宿舍的四个女生就来应征了。她们写了一封信，信中约这几位男士于三月三十一日晚十一时半到学校后面的花园9见面。见面时手拿鲜花，如果对方问：今天几号？回答为：明天是四月一号。

计算机系的这几个男生把信看了好几遍，不知道该不该去。因为四月一日就是西方的愚人节10，学生们都爱在这一天开别人的玩笑，说不定这几个女生也想拿他们开开心11。最后他们决定不去。几天以后，那几个女生又来了一封信，怪他们几个男生太没男子气12。她们说，如果真想交朋友，即使13别人开玩笑也应该勇敢地14接受15。

男生们赶快写了一封回信向女孩子们道歉16。周末17的时候，他们拿着鲜花去找那几个女生，请她们吃晚饭，女孩子们都非常高兴。晚饭后他们又一起去参加学校的周末舞会。不用说18，这个周末大家都过得很快乐。

（本文据《大学生》杂志某期报导改写）

查出或猜出空着的词：

1. 趣闻 anecdote
2. 某 [mǒu] a certain
3. 计算机 [jìsuànjī] computer
4. 男士 [nánshì] gentleman
5. 大方 natural easy-going, out-going
6. 善良 [shànliáng] kind-hearted
7. 应征 ________
8. 访 ________
9. 花园 ________
10. 愚人节 ________
11. 拿…开心 ________
12. 男子气 ________
13. 即使 [jíshǐ] even if
14. 勇敢地 [yǒnggǎn de] bravely
15. 接受 ________
16. 道歉 [dàoqiàn] apologize
17. 周末 ________
18. 不用说 ________

回答问题：

1.征友者是什么人？

2.征友者认为自己有些什么特点？对对方有什么要求？

3.启事上说应征者应该怎么与征友者联络？

4.应征者是什么人？是怎么应征的？约征友者怎么见面？

5.为什么征友者开始没有去与应征者见面？后来双方是怎么见面的？

（二）气功班招生

著名气功师赵金香教授将于下月在我校开办一期气功班。此套功简单易学、易练。每练一次只需二十分钟。学期为七天，每天一个半小时(晚6:30-8:00)。学费五十元，报名费二元。欲学者请速到我校报名并交费。

报名处：东二楼103室（李文新老师）报名时间：每天中午1:00-2:00

下面说的对不对？

1.这是一个公司的启事。

2.这个启事上说要开一个跟学校的课有关系的班。

3.这个班只开一个星期，每天半个小时。

4.要学的人得先交报名费和学费，一共五十元。

口语练习

I.回答问题：

1.你这个学期上几门课？你的课吃力吗？

2.什么课你需要找人辅导或补习？你觉得课外辅导有什么帮助？

3.你在学校怎么交朋友？有没有人用贴启事的方式？启事上怎么写？

II.谈谈你的看法：

请你谈谈学校的报纸上最近讨论的有关学生或学校的问题。

III.记者采访学生：

(三个学生一组，一个当学校报纸的记者，采访两个学生。)记者要问这两个学生对学校最近大家关心的一些事情的态度及看法。（请先选一个大家有兴趣的题目，做五分钟的准备，然后再开始练习。）

写作练习

1.请根据下面这段话写一个通知:

汉语中心外国留学生要开一个中国文化和西方文化的讨论会。要邀请有名的中国和外国学者来演讲（yǎnjiǎng: give a talk)和讨论。时间是这个月二十号下午两点半到五点。地点是在汉语中心大楼105室。欢迎其他同学和老师参加。

2.写采访报导：

上面〔口语练习〕里做了“记者采访”的练习。请把这次采访写成一篇报导。你可以从被采访的角度来谈，也可以从记者报导的角度来谈。

“真不想离开这个美丽的城市”

—旅游—

第十六课

语言情景　　语言结构　　文化介绍

It's vacation time for Dawei so he and some classmates take the opportunity to travel to some of China's most famous tourist attractions.

For our grammatical focus we continue to highlight forms of reduplication, this time learning how measure word reduplication permits more emphasis. We'll also show you how to express hypotheticals with 要不是…就….

Among the countless cultural sites in China, we focus on two of particular interest, Xi’an and Yungang.

“真不想离开这个美丽的城市”

-- 旅游 --

假期里，大为和几个留学生出去旅游。他们先乘火车到西安玩了两天，然后到南京，又由南京经成都最后到了昆明。这几个城市都各有各的特色，大为他们玩得很愉快。不过也许是因为昆明的天气最好，在那里待的时间也比较长，所以昆明给大为留下的印象很深。

昆明是位于中国西南的一个中型城市，也是云南省的省会，以气候温和闻名。有句话说，“万紫千红花不谢，冬暖夏凉四季春”，意思是这里一年四季都像春天一样，这就是为什么昆明也被人们叫作春城的缘故。当北京还在下大雪时，昆明已经开满鲜花了[i]。

i. “开满鲜花了”（"Flowers are in full bloom all over [the city]"). 满 ("full") is used here as a resultative verb ending suggesting that something [with boundary] has reached its fullest capacity within something else.

Examples:

屋子里坐满了人。	The room is fully seated [with people]. (...filled with people)
请你把杯子里倒满酒。	Please fill the cup with wine.
这张纸已经写满了。	This piece of paper has been filled (written fully).

美丽	美麗	měilì	ADJ/N beautiful; beauty
城市		chéngshì	N city(shortened as 市 after a name)
旅游	旅遊	lǚyóu	V/N to travel (for pleasure); tour/travel,
假期		jiàqī	N vacation (period)
愉快		yúkuài	ADJ/A happy; happily
乘		chéng	CV [formal] by (means of transportation) (syn. of 坐)
西安		Xī'ān	PW (name of city in China)
南京		Nánjīng	PW (name of city in China)
由		yóu	CV from (lit. form of 从)
经过	經過	jīngguò	CV by way of, via (can be shortened as 经)
成都		Chéngdū	PW (name of city in China)
各		gè	PRON/A each
特色		tèsè	N special (attractive) features
昆明		Kūnmíng	PW (name of city in China)
位于	位於	wèiyú	V [formal] be located at
-型		-xíng	BF -size; -type (used as N. suf.)
省		shěng	N province
云南省	雲南省	Yúnnán shěng	PW (name of province in China)
省会	省會	shěnghuì	N capital of a province (首都 is used for a country)
闻名	聞名	wénmíng	ADJ be well-known
气候	氣候	qìhòu	N climate
紫		zǐ	ADJ purple
谢	謝	xiè	V (of a flower) to wither and fade
冬天		dōngtiān	N winter
暖和		nuǎnhuo	ADJ (temperature) warm (in winter and spring)
夏天		xiàtiān	N summer
凉快	涼快	liángkuài	ADJ cool and comfortable (in summer and fall)
季节	季節	jìjié	N season (shortened as 季 in 四季、春季)
下雪		xià//xuě	VO to snow
开花	開花	kāi//huā	VO to blossom
满	滿	mǎn	ADJ be full

昆明的风景吸引了很多中外游客，特别是有名的西山和滇池风景区。爬上高高的西山龙门往下看滇池，真是再美不过了！远远地看去，滇池上一只只的小船像一片片的叶子，在湖上漂来漂去；阳光照在湖面上，湖水一闪一闪的[ii]，真像神话中的世界。

到了滇池的边上，你会发现这里又是一个新世界：云南民族村。因为云南有二十多个少数民族，政府就在滇池边上建了一个民族村，好让外来的人参观他们的民族文化。这些民族不但语言不同，而且生活方式也各种各样。他们都穿着花花绿绿的衣服，头上身上也有很多装饰品，漂亮极了。

昆明以南还有一个世界闻名的风景区，叫作石林。那里到处都是长得各种各样的石头，有的像人，有的像动物，有的像树，有的像花。你到了那里，就好像到了一个奇怪的石头王国。......

在昆明一个星期的旅游和参观使大为增长了不少知识，要不是因为该回北京上课了[iii]，他还真不想离开这个美丽的城市！

ii. “一闪一闪的” ("flickering") is another type of verb reduplication, indicating a repetitive motion or appearance of an action. The reduplicated verb achieves an effect of vividness. Note that verbs which suggest durative/ongoing actions or states (e.g.,睡、躺、说、看、玩） are not normally used in this structure.

Some examples of verb reduplication:

我的头怎么这么疼？一跳一跳的。Why do I have such a bad headache? It's pulsing.

这条鱼的嘴一张一张的，说明还没死。The fish's mouth keeps moving, which means it is still alive.

iii. 要不是因为该回北京上课了，他还不想离开这个美丽的城市 ("If it had not been time to go back to Beijing for classes, he would not have left this beautiful city"). This pattern (要不是...就...) permits the formation of hypotheticals (Were it not for.../Had it not been for.../If it had not been ..., etc.). See Focusing on Structure and Sentence Patterns and Expressions for additional examples.

风景	風景	fēngjǐng	N scenery,landscape
吸引		xīyǐn	V to attract, be appealing to
游客	遊客	yóukè	N tourist, traveler
池		chí	N pond, small lake
滇池		Diānchí	PW (name of a lake in Kunming, China)
爬		pá	V to climb, crawl
远远地	遠遠地	yuǎnyuǎnde	A (do...) from a distance
片		piàn	M piece, slice,etc.
叶子	葉子	yèzi	N leaf (of a tree) (shortened as 叶 after a name)
湖		hú	N lake
漂		piāo	V to drift, float (on water)
阳光	陽光	yángguāng	N sunlight
照		zhào	V to shine, illuminate
闪	閃	shǎn	V to sparkle, flash
建		jiàn	V to build, establish
民族		mínzú	N ethnicity(shortened as 族 after a name)
村		cūn	N village
少数	少數	shǎoshù	N the minority
政府		zhèngfǔ	N government
方式		fāngshì	N style (of doing something)
花花绿绿	花花綠綠	huāhuā lǜlǜ	PHR in bright, "loud" colors
...以南		...yǐ nán	PW to the south of...
石林		Shílín	PW Stone Forest (name of a scenic place)
石头	石頭	shítou	N stone, rock
王国	王國	wángguó	N kingdom
增长	增長	zēngzhǎng	V to grow,increase
知识	知識	zhīshi	N knowledge, learning

回答问题：

1. 大为他们这次旅游到过哪几个城市？
2. 昆明为什么也叫作春城？
3. 昆明有些什么吸引人的地方？
4. 为什么政府要在昆明建一个民族村？民族村有么特色？
5. “石林”是什么地方？有什么特色？
6. 为什么大为不想离开昆明？

语言结构

Focusing on Structure

I. Measure words can be reduplicated to emphasize each individual unit.

E.g.一天一天 ("day after day"),一个一个 "one after another". The form most often used is 一 M.一 M., but the second 一 is sometimes omitted. Examples:

一 M.(一) M.的 + Noun

湖上一只（一）只的小船就象一片（一）片的叶子，漂来漂去。
Boat after boat on the lake look just like leaves, drifting about.
这一本（一）本的中文书都是我买的。
All these Chinese books [one after another] were bought by me.
风一来，一张（一）张的纸都被吹到地上去了。
As the wind started,the paper was blown to the floor one sheet after another.

Noun 一 M. (一) M.地 + Verb

树上的叶子一片（一）片地掉了。
Leaves fell from the tree, one after another.
时间一天（一）天地过去了，可是信还是没有来。
Time passed day upon day, but the letter still didn't arrive.
房子着火了，人们一个（一）个地忙着从窗户往外跳。
The house caught fire, and people hurriedly jumped out of the window one after another.
她把刚买的衣服一件(一)件地拿出来给我看。
One after another she showed me the clothes she had just bought.

II. "要不是……" Subjunctive Sentences with "Yào bú shì..."

要不是 ... sentences are used to express hypothetical situations. The first part of the sentence (situation following 要不是) indicates the reality, and the second half of the sentence suggests the hypothetical situation. An adverb such as,还,就,or 真 etc., is usually used in the second part of the sentence to express various tones. If the sentence conveys the hypothetical viewed from the past, 不会 is often used in the second part for negation, instead of 没.
Examples:

昨天要不是（因为）下雨，我们就会出去玩了。

If it had not been raining (Had it not been raining) yesterday, we would have gone out to have fun.

The reality was that it WAS raining, therefore we did NOT go out to have fun (as desired).

要不是（因为）他有工作经验，那家公司还不会雇他呢。（ It is wrong to say 没雇他）
If it had not been for his work experience, that company would not have hired him yet.
Note: for the second part in the sentence above, 就不会...了 can also be used to convey the same message with a slightly different tone.

词汇用法

Word Usage

Verbs

- 旅游：出国旅游；到中国旅游；旅游期间；我喜欢旅游。/旅客/旅游者(tourist)
- 吸引：吸引游客(顾客、人的注意...)；她很吸引人(Adj)。
- 乘：乘车(船、飞机、火车...)；乘火车到上海；没乘过船；乘客(passenger)
- 照：阳光照在湖面上；灯光照得我眼睛很不舒服。/把房间照得很亮
- 建：建一个公司(国家、学校、楼...)；把民族村建在这里。/建得很早
- 漂：漂来漂去；漂在水上；湖上漂着几只小船。/叶子在水上漂着。
- 闪：灯光闪了一下。/湖水在阳光下一闪一闪的。/灯光在房间里闪着。
- 爬：在地上爬；爬山(墙)；爬得很高；慢慢地爬过来了
- 增长：增长知识（学问）；他的知识增长了很多。/ 这里的人口(population)增长得很快。

Verb-Object Compounds

- 下雪：下大雪；刚才下过一场雪。/雪下得很大。/下雪天
- 开花：春天是开花的季节。/开了很多花；这个花昨天刚开，今天就谢了。

Resultative Verb Compounds

- V满：坐满、倒满、写满、装满、贴满、挂满、住满、放满、(花)开满...
  教室里坐满了学生。/屋子里的人多是多，可是还没坐满。
  那张纸上写满了中国字。/盒子里装满了糖。
  墙上挂满了(贴满了)中国画。/这个地区住满了中国人。
  桌上放满了书和报。/花园里开满了各种各样的花。

Nouns

- 假期：新年假期；假期里；假期很长；我每年有两次假期。
- 特色：这个城市的特色；这个地方没什么特色。/这个大学很有特色(Adj)。
- 气候：气候很好；气候温和；这里的气候怎么样？
- 方式：生活(学习、做事、说话...)方式；不同的方式；他的生活方式很有特色。

Adjectives

- 愉快：我今天很愉快。/玩（学、谈、工作）得很愉快；祝你假期愉快！
- 闻名：中国菜(这本书、这个人、这个地方...)世界闻名。/他是一个全校闻名的人。
- 远远地：（前面）远远地走过来一个人。/从这里远远地看去，船像叶子一样小。

Others

- 片：一片叶子；一片姜；两片黄瓜；几片饼干；一片片的雪花(snowflakes)
- -型：大型城市；新型汽车；他是一个社交型的人，不是事业型的。

句型和习惯用语

Sentence Patterns and Expressions

1. 由A经B到C **(From A via B to C) [formal/written style]**

- 他们由南京经成都最后到了昆明。

  From Nanjing they passed through Chengdu and finally arrived in Kunming.
- 由台北开车经台中到台南，大概需要四个小时。
- 由____________经_______________到学校去，一路上可以看到很多商店。

2. (building, city...)位于...... **(... is located at...) [formal style]**

- 电脑中心位于图书馆的左边。

  The Computer Lab is located to the left of the library.
- 邮局位于学校和银行的中间。
- New York is a big city located in the eastern part of the United States. (*one single sentence*)

3....以......闻名 **(sth.\ sb.is famous for...) [formal style]**

- 昆明以气候温和闻名。 Kunming is famous for its mild climate.
- 这个学校以老师严格闻名。
- 甲：你们那个地方以什么闻名？乙: ______________________________
- Guangzhou is not only noted for their Cantonese cuisine, but also well known for flowers.

4.当A还在......时，B已经......了 **(When A is/was still..., B already...)**

- 当北京还在下大雪时，昆明已经开满鲜花了。
  When it is still snowing in Beijing, flowers are already in full bloom all over Kunming.
- 当你还在为那件事生气时，他已经把什么都忘了。
- 当我还在＿＿＿＿＿＿＿＿＿＿，他已经＿＿＿＿＿＿＿＿＿＿＿＿
- When you were still busy posting the "Dancing Party" notices, I had already notified all my classmates by phone.

5........,好让...... **(Sb. did sth. in order for sb. to ...\ ... so that sb. could ...)**

- 我把大门打开，好让客人把车子开进来。
  I opened the gate, so that the guest could drive in.
- 他给了我一本商业字典，好让我熟悉商业术语。
- 他带着我在附近看了看，＿＿＿＿＿＿＿＿＿＿＿＿＿＿＿＿＿＿＿＿
- I invited them to my birthday party in order for them to get to know each other.

6........各V各的...... **([plural items] each V. their own ...)**

- 这几个城市各有各的特色。 These cities each have their own attraction.
- 他喜欢吃肉而我喜欢吃素菜，所以我们各吃各的（饭）。
- 他和太太喜欢看的电视不一样，所以家里有两个电视机，＿＿＿＿＿＿＿。
- After the movies, we each went our own homes.

7.要不是（因为）(reality) ......，还.....（呢）\就 (counter-reality)......了

(But for the fact..., sb. would \would have done...)

- 要不是因为该回北京上课了，大为还真不想离开这个美丽的城市（呢）。
  If it had not been time to go back to Beijing for classes, David wouldn't have left this pretty city yet.
- 要不是（因为）我的钱不够，我就买了那所房子了。(我想买那所房子，可是我的钱不够，所以没有买。\如果我的钱够，我就买了）
- ________________________________，我到现在还不知道这件事呢。
- 要不是为了你,他 ________________________________到美国来了。
- If I had not posted that "Friends Wanted" notice, the two of us would have not met, let alone gotten married.

Convert 要不是 to 要是 or 如果 by reversing the fact of the first half of the sentence to achieve the same effect.

Example:

要不是(因为)我的钱不够 -->要是我的钱够,....

要不是(因为)你告诉我-->________________________________

文化介绍

Learning About Culture

中国文化名胜

Chinese Cultural/Historical Sites

With a written history of over two thousand years, China has countless interesting cultural sites. The places discussed below are just two examples.

Xī'ān (西 安), the capital of Shǎnxī (陕 西) province, was called Cháng'ān (长安) in ancient times. It was the capital of eleven imperial dynasties for more than eleven hundred years. As a result, there are many historical sites that make for interesting visits. The most facinating of all is the tomb of the first emperor of China, 221-209 B.C. (秦始皇陵). The very size of this tomb is impressive, measuring about two hundred and sixty feet high, five hundred yards from east to west, and four hundred and eighty yards from north to south. It can be seen from a long way off. Unearthed from one of the subordinate tombs are six thousand lifelike terracotta warriors, ranging from five to six feet in height, each with a different facial expression. In addition to these warriors there are also thousands of life-size chariots and saddled horses.

For people who are interested in the arts, Yúngāng (云岗) is the place to see. These stone cave Buddhist temples are located sixteen kilometers west of the city of Dàtóng (大同), Shānxī (山西) province. The caves are hollowed out of a mountain and the temples are built into and above them. In the caves are over 51,000 statues. Stretching for about one kilometer from east to west, Yúngāng is one of the largest stone cave temple structures in China.

Work on these caves began some fifteen hundred years ago.Twenty-one major caves have been discovered so far. The caves have been a subject of study for hundreds of years. It is believed that Yúngāng marks a crucial period in the history of Chinese art. Countless influences from central Asian culture can be seen in the works of these caves. Yúngāng is one of the finest examples of Chinese Buddhist sculpture.

第十六课听力练习

第一部分：单句

请你们听下面的句子。每个句子的意思是什么？请在三个选择中选出一句来。

1. (a)从这里坐火车到波士顿，要不要经过纽约？
   (b)从这里到波士顿，坐火车要多少时间？
   (c)从波士顿到纽约，坐火车要多少时间？

2. (a)学生餐厅在电脑中心的右边。
   (b)学生餐厅和电脑中心都在右边。
   (c)学生餐厅的右边是电脑中心。

3. (a)这个城市的风景不怎么美。
   (b)这个城市有一个很美的名字。
   (c)这个城市因为风景很美，所以很有名。

4. (a)他们和我们在同一个时间放假。
   (b)他们考试的时候我们已经放假了。
   (c)他们放假的时候我们还在为考试忙着呢。

5. (a)他为了让我们看清楚启事上的字，所以把灯打开。
   (b)灯光照得我们看不清楚启事上的字。
   (c)他不让我们开灯，所以我们看不清楚启事上的字。

6. (a)要是外头下大雪，他就不愿意待在家里。
   (b)因为外头下大雪，所以他愿意在家里待着。
   (c)因为外头下大雪，所以他不想待在家里。

7. (a)计算机太贵了，所以我不能再买一个。
   (b)计算机就是不贵，我也不想再买一个。
   (c)计算机虽然不便宜，但是我又买了一个。

第二部分：对话

第一遍:下面是小吴和小林的对话。请你们听懂这个对话的大意，然后回答问题。

问题：小吴和小林主要在说些什么？

a)关于旅游的事　　b)关于参观博物馆的事

第二遍:请你们读下面的句子，然后把这个对话再听一次。听完后，看看这些句子说得对不对。

_____1.小林今年春假想去爬山。

_____2.小吴和她男朋友已经决定到纽约去玩了。

_____3.小吴的男朋友希望春假期间能在旧金山(San Francisco)待几天。

_____4.小吴比较想到纽约去玩。

第三遍:请你们读下面的问题，然后听第三遍。听完后，请回答问题。

1.小林今年春假打算怎么过？

a)去爬山　　b)到海边玩　　c)待在家里休息

2.小吴的男朋友想到什么地方去过春假？

a)美国南部　　b)旧金山　　c)纽约

3.小吴的男朋友觉得旧金山怎么样？

a)风景很美　　b)住满了中国人　c)使人觉得不愉快

4.小吴为什么想到纽约去？

a)因为纽约以气候温和闻名　b)因为纽约很有文化

c)因为纽约的风景很漂亮

5.小林给小吴出了什么主意？

a)小林要小吴跟她的男朋友去旧金山玩。

b)小林觉得小吴应该想办法让她的男朋友跟她去纽约。

c)小林认为小吴和她的男朋友的看法如果不能统一，那他们就只好各去一个城市了。

第十六课 练习
词汇；句型；语法

I.选择适当的词语:

	a.	b.	c.
1.我今年有两次______。	a.放假	b.假期	c.节日
2.____北京到西安的火车马上就要开了。	a.由	b.离	c.至
3.这个城市很有_______。	a.特别	b.特色	c.风景
4.成都_______是四川省的省会。	a.城市	b.市	c.城
5.你是哪一个_____去北京的？	a.季	b.季节	c.四季
6.那个地区的_____很温和。	a.气候	b.风景	c.特色
7.他是一个世界______的学者。	a.很有名	b.闻名	c.都知道
8.水上有一个东西在_____。	a.照	b.漂	c.亮
9.我很喜欢他们的生活_____。	a.式	b.型	c.方式
10.屋子里的灯光____了一下就不亮了。	a.闪	b.照	c.开
11.路灯_____亮了前面的巷子。	a.闪	b.照	c.开
12.旅游可以使人_______知识。	a.长大	b.加	c.增长
13.花只开了三天就_____了。	a.满	b.谢	c.开满
14.刚才突然下大雨了，__我穿了雨衣。	a.好让	b.好在	c.要不是
15.我们学校位____市中心。	a.于	b.在	c.与
16.______你打电话给我，我还不知道你来了呢。	a.既然	b.要不是	c.好在

II.用“V满”的适当形式填空：

1.我们去晚了，屋子里已经__________了，所以我们只好站在外面了。

2.那个书架还没____________，你可以把书放到那儿去。

3.这个箱子太大，装了这么多的东西，还是________________。

4.春天的时候他家的花园里_____________各种鲜花，漂亮极了。

5.我喜欢画，我家里的墙上、门上都_____________了画。

6.中秋节的晚上，家家的桌子上都____________了好吃的东西。

III.用适当的量词重叠式填空(一片片、一个个......)

1.征友启事刚贴出去不久，应征的信就__________地来了。

2.秋天的时候，树上的叶子都__________地掉到了地上。

3.你怎么把我给你买的衣服__________地都给了人了？

4.他把我买的啤酒__________地都喝完了。

5.冬天到了，鸟都__________飞到南方去了。

6.我们班的同学毕业以后都__________出国了。

IV.用“要不是......”改写下面的句子：

例子：如果那本书太贵，我当时就不会买了。

--->要不是（因为）那本书便 宜，我就不会买了。

(请先复习句型，再作下面的句子)

1.如果他不告诉我那个地方，我就一定不会想到去那里旅游了。

2.他到那个少数民族地区去，是为了了解那里的文化、增长知识。

3.虽然他不想离开英国，可是为了跟你在一起，所以他到这里来了。

4.因为你帮忙，所以我今天做完了这件事。

5.那家大公司雇用了他，是因为他既有能力又有经验的缘故。

阅读练习

历史名城西安

寒假1到了，我和弟弟都想借这个机会出去旅游一下，正好收到住在西安的叔叔的来信，说寒假期间可以到他那里去玩几天。我们高兴极了，马上买了火车票到西安来了。我们早就在上历史课的时候知道西安是个有名的古城，中国的第一个皇帝就是在这里建都2的，后来又有十个朝代把西安作为首都3。可是"百闻不如一见4"，到了这里一看，才发现西安真是一个天然的5中国历史博物馆！到处都能看见古代建筑6，而且还有史前7文化 的遗址8。

西安市中心有一个有名的钟楼，建于明朝。楼上有一个5000公斤9的大铁钟10，所以叫作钟楼。在市区以东30公里的地方有一个风景区，叫作骊山11。骊是古代的一种马，据说骊山远看就像一匹骊马，所以称为骊山。骊山风景极美，同时又以温泉12闻名，所以自古13就是皇帝游玩的地方，这就是为什么这里有很多宫殿14式建筑的缘故。中国的皇帝不但生前要玩乐，死后也不愿寂寞，所以在生前很早就开始建筑自己的陵墓15，也就是自己死后住的地下宫殿。离骊山不远的地方就有中国第一个皇帝建的地下宫殿。在一个博物馆里，我们看到了在地下宫殿附近出土的6000多个兵马16俑17以及用金、银、等做的装饰品，真让我们看目瞪口呆18！吸引我们的还有市郊19的半坡村，这是一个6000年前留下来的村子，对我们了解史前文化很有帮助。

离开西安的头一天，叔叔一家又带我们去吃饺子宴20。这是西安最有名的一家饺子店，也可以说是全中国饺子做法最多的一家。大大小小，各种颜色，各种味道，各种包法，各种吃法（煮的、炸的、蒸的等等），据说有一百多种！每天都有很多中外游客来品尝这家的饺子店的饺子......

西安之游使我们增长了很多历史知识。当我们坐上火车回家的时候，我的眼前好像还有那一个个跟真人真马一样大小的兵马俑，和那一盘盘颜色、味道、形状21不同的饺子.......

词汇表（查出或猜出空着的词语的意思）：

1. 寒假 [hánjià] winter break	8. 遗址 [yízhǐ] ruins	15. 陵墓 [língmù] tomb
2. 建都 _______________	9. 公斤 [gōngjīn] kilogram	16. 兵马 [bīng mǎ] soldiers and horses
3. 首都 [shǒudū] capital of a country	10. 铁钟 [tiě zhōng] iron bell	17. 俑 [yǒng] terra-cotta figurine
4. 百闻不如一见_________	11. 骊山 [Líshān] (name)	18. 目瞪口呆___________
5. 天然的_____________	12. 温泉 ___________	19. 市郊 [shìjiāo] suburb
6. 建筑 [jiànzhù] architecture	13. 自古 from ancient times	20. 宴 [yàn] banquet
7. 史前 _____________	14. 宫殿 [gōngdiàn] palace	21. 形状 _____________

下面哪一句对？

1. a.西安是历史名城，主要以史前文化闻名。
   b.西安是历史名城，中国有十一个朝代把这里作为都城。

2. “百闻不如一见”的意思是：
   a.自己看见一次比听别人说一百次好。
   b.别人说的不一定对，不应该相信。

3. a.中国皇帝喜欢到骊山游玩，因为那里有温泉和美丽的风景。
   b.骊山的风景极美，所以皇帝在那里建了很多地下宫殿，好让自己玩乐。

4. a.皇帝的地下宫殿是在皇帝出生以前开始建的。
   b.一个皇帝活着的时候就开始建自己的陵墓。

5. a.市郊的半坡村出土了六千个兵马俑，跟真人真马一样大小。
   b.半坡村可以使人们了解到中国六千年前的一些文化。

6. a.西安的一家饺子店以饺子做法多闻名。
   b.西安的饺子好吃，全国闻名。

口语练习

I.回答问题：

1.你喜欢旅游吗？你去过哪些地方？
2.你觉得哪个地方给你的印象最深？为什么？它跟别的地方有什么不同？
3.你觉得你最想住在什么地方？为什么？

II. 描述一个地方：

a.练习方位词：东南、西南、东北、西北；美国东部、美国的东边；这个城市以东是...；

b.说一下你所在的地方位于哪里？它的周围(*zhōuwéi*: surroundings)是些什么地方？

c.请介绍一下你最喜欢的一个地方（在哪里 、气候、风景、文化特色）

III. 作比较：谈谈你熟悉的两个城市各有什么特点？

(Use the worksheet below for your preparation notes)

	城市一	城市二
在哪个国家、什么地方（____部）		
气候特点		
以什么闻名（博物馆、建筑物、产品、历史、风景 ...）		
文化特点（风俗习惯、生活方式）		

有用的词语和句型

以......闻名
像......这样的____
除了......以外，也......
据......所V
这就是（为什么）......的缘故
要不是......，就（不）会......了
在......方面，......
A跟B很相似/很不同；
A......，而B却......
A没有B那么......；
A比B更......

写作练习

<u>请选一题</u>：

1.请你描写一下你的家乡　　　　2.介绍一个地方

<u>你的作文应该包括以下几个方面</u>：

—这个地方在哪里（位于...）；

—靠近什么地方（附近是什么地方）（东边、南边、以北、西北....等等）

—四季气候的特点

—以什么闻名（出什么东西、有什么吸引人的地方，等等）

—文化上有什么特色（人、风俗习惯、对什么感兴趣）

—什么方面给你印象最深/你觉得什么方面最有意思

"你们的价格是否可以降低一点？"

—贸易洽谈—

第十七课

语言情景　　语言结构　　文化介绍

Here, in Lesson 17, you join Hailin as she participates in a trade negotiation between her boss and a foreign businessman. We take the opportunity to learn about the kind of language used in formal situations such as this one.

Our structural segment presents a very important feature of Chinese: the whole before the part principle. You'll learn that this principle (quite the opposite of English, by the way) influences many expressions in Chinese.

And culturally, you will learn a bit about the special etiquette that pertains during a business conversation (贸易洽谈).

"你们的价格是否可以降低一点？"

--贸易洽谈--

海琳在进出口公司工作了好几个月了，她已经熟悉了自己的业务，并且跟同事们也相处得很好。她每天的工作都很忙，不但要处理很多货单和商业资料，而且有时还要和外商进行贸易洽谈，这也是她最喜欢做的事。这一天又有一个外商来谈订货的事，海琳也参加了。

（一）

外商：赵先生，我们对贵公司的产品很有兴趣，其中有几项我们需要量很大。我们想知道你们的价格是否ⁱ可以再降低一点？

i. 是否 is used in the formal style to form a choice-type question with the verb 是 followed by the main verb of the sentence. Examples:

他是否是中国人？（=是不是）
你们是否订购这种产品？（=是不是订购;订购不订购）
你们是否能给我们一点折扣？(=是不是能;能不能；also 能否）
我们是否可以明天付款？（=是不是可以;可以不可以；also 可否）

贸易	貿易	màoyì	N (large scale) trade
洽谈	洽談	qiàtán	V/N[formal] to negotiate (business); negotiation
同事		tóngshì	V/N to work at the same place/co-worker, colleague
相处	相處	xiāngchǔ	V to be together [w/sb.] for a period of time
处理	處理	chǔlǐ	V to handle, process, take care of (a matter)
单子	單子	dānzi	N list
货单	貨單	huòdān	N inventory, order form ("list of merchandise")
资料	資料	zīliào	N data, written information
进行	進行	jìnxíng	V to proceed (to), carry on (with)
订	訂	dìng	V to place an order; make a reservation
贵	貴	guì	BF [court.] your distinguished...
贵公司	貴公司	guì gōngsī	NP your distinguished company
贵方	貴方	guìfāng	NP your side (the opposite party in a negotiation)
是否		shìfǒu	QW whether or not (lit. form of 是不是) (See Note i.)
降低		jiàngdī	V/RV to lower, bring down (price, standard, etc.)

赵经理：关于[ii]这个问题，我们可以商量。我想您大概也知道我们的产品价格在国际市场上都很有竞争性。所以除非您的订货量大，否则我们一般是不给折扣的。

外商：这一点我理解。请您看一下这个单子，上面就是我们准备订购的货物，前两项如果价格合适，我们准备各订购两万件，其他几项各五千。我们希望能得到百分之五的折扣。

赵经理：先生，我们公司出口的产品质量非常可靠，价格也很合理，所以按照你的订货量，我们最多只能给您百分之二的折扣，这已经是现在市场上最低的价格了。

外商：赵先生，百分之二是否太少了点儿？我们是第一次跟你们订货，如果贵方能给我们更低一点的价格，我们今后还会长期合作，否则我们只好……

赵经理：这样好不好：VR-300型的电脑配件是新产品，我们不能再降了，其它的如果您每项再多[iii]订两千，那我们就给您百分之三点五的折扣，怎么样？这已经是低于[iv]市场价格了，您是不是也能做一点让步？

外商：好吧，那就这样吧。下面我们是不是谈一下付款方式？

赵经理：好的。

……

ii. 关于……（regarding...）关于 is often used to mark a topic to be discussed and normally takes the initial position in a sentence. It may also introduce a noun phrase which follows the verb. In either case, 关于 must precede the phrase being modified. Examples:

What's your opinion regarding studying abroad?
关于出国留学的事，你有什么看法？（NOT:你有什么看法关于出国留学？）
Yesterday I read some books about foreign trade.
我昨天看了一些关于外贸方面的书。（NOT:我昨天看了一些书关于外贸方面。）

iii. 多 can be placed before the verb to act as an adverb, meaning "[do] more". Note the difference in word order between Chinese and English in the following examples, especially when there is a quantified object.

你得多练习说话。You should practice speaking more (often).
我本来只想买两个，可是因为便宜，我多买了三个。..., I bought three more.

iv. 低于... means "lower than..." 于 is one of the most frequently used literary particles in formal or semiformal Chinese. Its meaning varies (e.g. at, in, from or than) according to the meaning of the word it is attached to.

他将于明早离美。He will leave America tomorrow morning.
他七五年生于北京。He was born in Beijing in 1975.
这个价格高于市场价格。This price is higher than the market price.

关于	關於	guānyú	CONJ/CV regarding,about, concerning (See Note ii.)
国际	國際	guójì	MOD international
市场	市場	shìchǎng	N market
竞争	競爭	jìngzhēng	V/N to compete; competition
量		liàng	N quantity, volume
折扣		zhékòu	N discount
订购	訂購	dìnggòu	V to order (for purchasing)
质量	質量	zhìliàng	N quality
可靠		kěkào	ADJ reliable
合作		hézuò	V/N to co-operate; do business with; co-operation
除非		chúfēi	MA unless
否则	否則	fǒuzé	CONJ otherwise
配件		pèijiàn	N parts, component (of a machine)
项	項	xiàng	M item (Measure Word for goods, topics, etc.)
-于	-於	-yú	V-SUF [lit] than (as in 低于)
让步	讓步	ràng//bù	VO to yield, compromise
付款		fù//kuǎn	VO to make payment

（二）

赵经理：吴小姐，请先别走，有一点事要跟你谈一下。

海琳：什么事？

赵经理：是这样：下个星期北京要举行一个外贸洽谈会。原来安排李先生跟我去参加，但是李先生有另外一个生意要谈。所以我们决定让你跟我一块儿去，怎么样？

海琳：什么？去北京？！我不是在做梦吧？

赵经理：你准备一下，我们下星期二就走。

海琳：谢谢赵经理！......啊—我要去北京了！！我得赶快打电话告诉大为！ ......不，还是不告诉他的好[v]，给他一个意外的惊喜！

v. “还是不告诉他的好”（"[On second thought], I think it's better not to tell him."）还是...的好 is used to indicate a decision made after comparing alternatives or weighing the situation.

做梦	做夢	zuò//mèng	VO to dream
意外		yìwài	ADJ/N unexpected, accidental; accident
惊喜	驚喜	jīngxǐ	N (delightful) surprise

判断出以下词语的意思：

外商	外商
竞争性	競爭性
订货量	訂貨量
原价	原價
今后	今後
长期	長期

回答问题：

1.海琳每天做些什么样的工作？她最喜欢做什么？

2.这个外商到公司来谈什么事？这笔生意谈成了没有？

3.赵经理通知海琳什么事？海琳听了以后觉得怎么样？她决定怎么做？

guo ji shi chang

语言结构

Focusing on Structure

The Whole-before-Part Principle

Generally speaking, Chinese sentences or phrases obey the whole-before- part principle, which is opposite from English and some other languages. That is, a term or phrase indicating the general or whole is usually placed before the term or phrase indicating the specific or part of the whole. We can take this principle metaphorically and consider the concept of whole as a "container" and the part as the "content[s]" or the contained. The usage patterns in the following provide examples:

A. Numerical units: The bigger contains the smaller. Hence, the denominator precedes the numerator, e.g.:

百分之五 (5%, five percent)
whole part

三分之二 (2/3, two thirds)
whole part

B. Groups vs. individuals: Group contains individual. For example, 各 (each) denotes "individual" or "part" of a group or whole, 各 therefore normally appears after the group or whole is present or stated.

这几种笔，请各（种）给我一枝。 Please give me one of each of these pens.
group individual

这两个城市，各有各的特色。Each of these two cities has its own attractions.
group individual

我们班的学生有的是外国人。Some of the students in our class are foreigners.
whole part

C. Time frames: The bigger unit contains the smaller unit

九六年二月五日 February 5, 1996; 今天早上九点 9 o'clock this morning

D. Place names: the larger unit contains the smaller unit

中国上海 Shanghai, China
中国北京学院路15号 15 Xueyuan Road, Beijing, China

词汇用法
Word Usage

Verbs

- 相处：跟人相处；我没跟他相处过。/相处了一段时间；相处得很好
- 处理：处理事情(问题、资料 ...)；处理得很好；没处理过这样的事情；你得赶快把这件事情处理了。/这件事我处理不好，还是你来吧。
- 进行：进行一个新计划(活动、洽谈...)；贸易洽谈(考试...)正在进行；进行了一段时间；进行得怎么样？/进行得很顺利(很慢)
- 订购：订购产品(书报、机票...)；订购一万件；向谁订购
- 合作：我喜欢跟他合作。/我们合作得很好。/合作了很多年(很多次)
- 竞争：我们跟他们竞争。/竞争得很厉害；竞争性很大
- 付：付款；付钱(房租、学费、定金...)；付过了；付完了

Verb-Object and Resultative-Verb Compounds

- 让步：他不愿意让步。/我已经让了很多步了。/请你做一点<u>让步</u>(N.)。
- 降低：降低价格(要求、生活水平...)；把价钱降低一点；已经降得很低了

Adjectives and Adverbs

- 可靠：可靠的牌子(人、说法...)；这个人(说法)不可靠。
- 长期：长期相处(合作...)；长期的努力

Nouns

- 折扣：打(给)折扣；打(给)了很多折扣；打(给)5%的折扣
- 质量：产品(工作、教学...)的质量；质量很高(可靠)；质量不好(很差)
- 生意：做生意；谈生意；生意谈得很顺利。/很大的一笔生意；生意人
- 惊喜：给他一个惊喜；意外的惊喜
- 贸易：做贸易；贸易公司(洽谈、中心...)；国际贸易；贸易商

Measure Words

- 项：一项计划；一项活动；一项新产品

Prefixes and Suffixes

- 可-：可靠；可爱；可信；可怕......
- 单：货(订、菜、名...)单；公司接到很多订（货）单。/请给我一份菜单。/学生名单上没有你的名字。

Others

- 各：这几样东西，我想各买(拿、订购...)一个。/这几个大学(地方、人...)各有各的特色。
- 于：低于市场价格（三千元）；少于二十人；高于美国的生活水平；晚于三点

句型和习惯用语

Sentence Patterns and Expressions

1.是否……**(Is it...or not? Do/Does ...or not?) [formal style]**

- 不知道那个公司产品的质量是否可靠？

  I wonder whether the quality of that company's products is reliable.
- 你是否参观过那个博物馆？
- 甲：____？

  乙：这已经是最低价格了，不能再降了。
- I wonder whether they are getting along well.

2.关于……的 **(N.) (regarding.../concerning.../about...) (See Note ii)**

- 我想谈谈关于出国留学方面的事情/问题。 I'd like to talk about studying abroad.
- 关于中国的传统习惯，我一点也不了解。

  I don't know anything about Chinese customs.
- 他对关于____事很感兴趣。
- He wrote a book concerning the current situation in China.

3.除非……否则…… **(unless..., otherwise...)**

- 除非您的订货量大，否则我们一般是不给折扣的。

  Generally we don't give discounts unless you place a large order.
- 除非父母给我钱，否则我不可能上这个学校。
- 除非工作时间灵活，____
- I won't buy it unless you lower the price a little bit.

4. 多 **Verb (quantity).... ([do] more...) (See Note iii)**

- 今天的人很多，你多做一点菜。

  We have many people here today, please make more food.
- 我知道你也想买这本书，所以就多买了一本。
- 做完练习以后，__________________________你就检查得出你的错来了。
- When you make soup, always add more salt.

5. ....,还是......的好。**(I think [upon reflection] that it is better for me [you, him, etc.] to do...) (See Note v)**

- 今天雪太大，我们还是不出去的好。

  The snowfall is heavy today. Maybe it's better that we stay home.
- 如果你想减肥的话，还是多吃素菜的好。
- 他没有什么经验，我看这件事还是你去〔办〕的好。
- 甲：我既想学中文又想学日文，你看到底学什么好？

  乙：各有各的好处。如果我是你 的话，我看__________________________
- I think it's better that I find a tutor and brush up on my Chinese before I go travel in China.

文化介绍

Learning About Culture

语言客套

Formalities In Various Kinds Of Writing

In every kind of situation, whether official, business, or social, the Chinese, more so than Americans, use conventional language, often in the form of stock phrases. In business transactions, personal pronouns are avoided. When reference is made to the second party, guì gōngsī, 贵公司 "your honorable company, factory, organization, etc." is used; when to oneself, bì gōngsī 敝公司 or běn gōngsī 本公司, "the humble, or this, company, factory, etc." In addition, to show respect for the second party, business negotiations or letters use circumlocutions such as kěfǒu 可否 "can or cannot," shìfǒu 是否 "is or is not," etc., when the speaker or writer seeks the views of the person to whom he is talking/writing.

In written reports, essays, or even the preface of a book, certain stock phrases are present. Conventional language includes the following phrases:

我的准备不够。

(My preparation for presenting this has not been sufficient.)

我的书里有不少错误，敬请多多包涵/原谅。

(There are many mistakes in my work. I would like to ask for your forgiveness.)

欢迎各位批评指教！

(I welcome your criticism and corrections)

第十七课听力练习

第一部分：单句

请你们听下面的句子。每个句子的意思是什么？请在三个选择中选出一句来。

1. (a)那件事你是不是已经处理好了？
(b)那件事是你处理的吗？
(c)你想不想把那件事处理好？

2. (a)我不知道他们是不是有趣的生意人。
(b)我不知道他们想不想跟我们做生意。
(c)我不知道他们喜欢不喜欢做生意。

3. (a)他的兴趣跟国际贸易有关。
(b)关于国际贸易的事，他没有兴趣。
(c)他想学习国际贸易方面的事。

4. (a)他有很多旅游方面的书。
(b)他旅行的时候喜欢买书。
(c)他一边旅行一边看书。

5. (a)你得让步他才愿意跟你合作。
(b)你就是让步，他也不愿意跟你合作。
(c)要不是你作了让步，他才不会跟你合作。

6. (a)明天就是下大雪，火车也一定准时开。
(b)不管明天下不下雪，火车都不开。
(c)如果明天不下雪，火车一定准时开。

7. (c)这家商店的毛衣不便宜，所以我只买了一件。
(b)这家商店的毛衣每件只要五块钱，所以我买了很多件。
(a)这家商店的毛衣卖得比以前便宜，所以我多买了一件。

8. (a)感冒的时候应该喝水喝得比平时多。
(b)感冒的时候应该开始喝水。
(c)感冒的时候不必喝太多水。

第二部分：短文

第一遍:请你们听懂这篇短文的大意，然后回答问题。

问题：海琳和她的同事星期六下午做了什么事？

a)参加外贸洽谈会

b)到百货公司去买东西

第二遍:请你们读下面的句子，然后把这篇短文再听一次。听完后，看看这些句子说得对不对。

_____1.海琳一想到要去北京开会就开心极了。

_____2.海琳写了一封信跟大为说这件事，好让大为也高兴高兴。

_____3.海琳趁着百货公司打折的时候去给大为和她自己买礼物。

_____4.海琳是和她的同事小杨一块去买东西的。

_____5.海琳他们买的衣服质量比较低，所以特别便宜。

第三遍:请你们把最后一段再听一遍。听完后，在左边的空格中填入合适的选择。(Listen to the last paragraph, and then match the person with the correct information.)

_____海琳　　a.买了几样化妆品

　　　　　　b.买了一条长裙

_____小杨　　c.给自己买了两件衬衫

　　　　　　d.买了一条灰长裤

　　　　　　e.没买长裤

第十七课 练习
词汇；句型；语法

I.填空：

1.相处：我____他相处了_______，我们相处得_______。他很_______相处。

2.资料：我今天有很多资料需要____________。/他给我们提供了很多_________。/我现在正在研究中国历史，每天都到图书馆去_______。

3.产品：__________产品；产品质量__________；这个公司的________产品特别受欢迎。

4.进行：___________正在进行。/上次的讨论_____________很顺利。

5.合作：我跟他们_____________几次，我们____________很顺利。将来我们还会在______________________进行合作。

6.降/降低：学生觉得老师太严格了，希望老师__________________。/这个产品从$50______$30，已经______很低了，不能再______了。

7.可-：这个人是我的朋友，他做事很_________。/你的小孩眞_________。/他说的话很___________。/那个人满脸都是血，___________极了！

8.关于：我们刚才在讨论________________________。/你写的书是不是关于_______的？ /关于____________________________，我们需要再商量一下才能做决定。

II.完成句子：

1.晚会以后，大家就____________________________________（各V各的N）

2.我去过很多地方，这些地方______________________________（各V....）

3.这几种贺年卡我都很喜欢，我想 ______________________ (各V+quantity)

4.我想了解一下你们公司 ____________________________（是否......）

5.他们要找一个负责北美市场的业务经理。________________________
____(除非......，否则......)

6.________________________________，我想谈谈我的看法。(关于)

7.关于假期到哪里去旅游的事情，我看 ______________（还是......的好）

阅读练习

1.商业信函：请读下面的商业信函并回答问题。（划线地方为商业信函的常用语。）(Read the following business letter and then answer the questions. The underlined phrases are conventional usages)

敬启者：

最近我们有机会参观了台北国际贸易展览会，对贵公司产品的高品质及低廉价格留下了深刻印象。

本公司现为台北最大的食品贸易公司之一，在台湾各主要城市设有办事处和代理商。过去几年中我们已从美国进口大量食品及饮料，故在食品进口及推销方面有丰富经验。我们相信贵公司的产品一定会在台湾有良好销路。

如果贵公司愿与本公司建立贸易关系，我们将甚为感激。期盼您的回音。

xxx 敬上

回答问题：

1.这封信是什么公司写的？公司在什么地方？他们主要做什么方面的贸易？

2.信是写给哪国的公司的？他们是从哪里知道这家公司的？为什么会对这家公司的产品感兴趣？

3.写信的公司认为自己的公司有什么优势？他们希望做什么？为什么他们想这样做？

2.商业广告：请看下面的广告并回答问题。

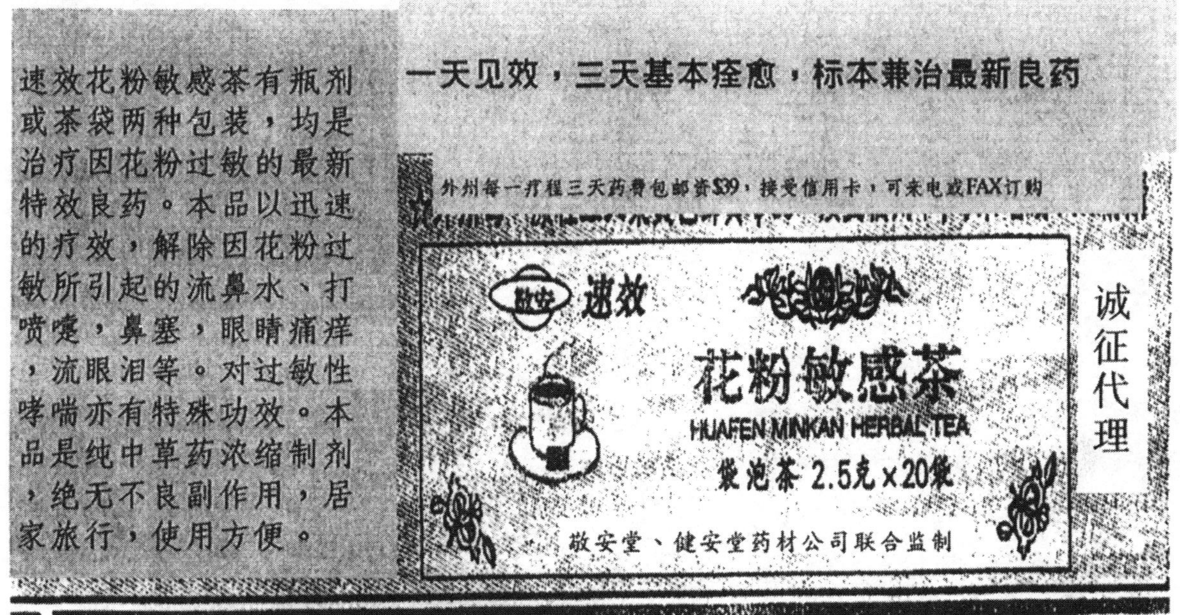

回答问题：

1. 这个广告推销的"花粉敏感茶"对什么有效？

2. 这种"敏感茶"是用什么做的？有什么特点？

3. 产品是怎么包装的？

4. 这种中药茶需要喝多久？

5. 怎么买这种中药茶？

6. 敏感茶要多少钱？可以用什么方式付款？

口语练习

I. 熟读下面的数字单位：（从右到左）

（亿 万千 万百 万十 万 千 百 十 个）

II. 练习快速读出下面的数字并加上后面的名词：

a.	54.2	54.2%	54.02%	（产品）
b.	1/2	3/10	2/5	（学生）
c.	2002	2020	2200	（电视机/台）
d.	20,002	20,020	22,000	（电脑：部/台）
e.	220,000	200,200	202,000	（汽车：部/辆）
f.	2,500,000	25,000,000	250,000,000	（美元）

III. 请练习下面的贸易洽谈常用语:

*您是否可以......？（给我们一个报价(quotation)/一点折扣）

*能不能请您......？（把价格降低百分之...）

*我们希望贵方能...... （跟我们合作/进行进一步洽谈）

*如果......,那我们将......（尽快做出决定/使这笔生意成交 [make a deal]）

IV. 情景会话：贸易洽谈

你代表_____国的一家公司去台湾/大陆进行贸易商谈。你想推销_____国的一种新产品（如化妆品、电器、设备、药物、食品等等）。你先介绍这种产品的用处、好处、价格等等，然后想办法说服你的客户买你的产品。（请注意说话的语气和客套。）

写作练习

<u>写商业广告</u>：

请你选一种商品做广告。你的介绍应包括下面几个方面：

—产品的名称，产地

—这种产品的性能和特点（features）

—对什么人合适

—价格，购买方式

“我们喜欢中国！”

—欢送会—

第十八课

语言情景　　语言结构　　文化介绍

Here, in our last lesson, you join Dawei and his classmates as they conclude their studies and bid farewell to their teachers. It's Dawei that gets a chance to deliver the "farewell address" and you get a chance to learn about the conventions involved in speech-making (发言或演讲).

Structurally, you'll revisit the verb-到 form (first seen in Lesson 11) and learn more about its flexibility in forming many verbal expressions.

In the final cultural segment, you'll continue to see how the Chinese language uses conventional language and stock phrases to reflect such fundamental cultural values as modesty and self-deprecation.

"我们喜欢中国！"

--欢送会--

大为他们在北京的学习结束了，学校的汉语中心开欢送会庆祝他们顺利完成学习。会上，中心的负责人和老师代表都讲了话，鼓励留学生们回国后继续努力，将来为研究中国文化、为促进中西文化的交流做出贡献。大为他们几个留学生都很激动。

玛丽：欸，大为，雅克，我怎么今天有一种说不出来的感觉，不知道是想哭还是是想笑。

雅克：我可没有这种感觉，我只是觉得特别高兴，因为我就要回法国了！啊，一想到很快就可以吃到我最喜欢的东西我就兴奋得不得了。大为—你呢？

大为：我现在还来不及感觉什么，因为我马上就要上台讲话了，现在紧张得要命！

……

张老师：现在我们请李大为同学代表留学生讲话，大家欢迎！

大为：各位[i]老师、各位同学：谢谢你们给我这个机会代表留学生讲话。我今天很激动，没有准备好，讲得不好的地方请大家原谅。首先我要借这个机会代表留学生感谢汉语中心的领导、各位老师以及所有的工作

i. 各位...... is conventionally used in formal speech to address the audience.

欢送会	歡送會	huānsònghuì	N farewell party
结束	結束	jiéshù	V to end; (sth.) come to an end
讲话	講話	jiǎng//huà	VO/N to give speech, to talk; speech, talk
鼓励	鼓勵	gǔlì	V/N to encourage; encouragement
继续	繼續	jìxù	V to continue (doing)
将来	將來	jiānglái	PW/N in the future; future
促进	促進	cùjìn	V to promote (friendship, understanding, etc.)
交流		jiāoliú	N exchange (of culture, thoughts, etc.)
以及		yǐjí	CONJ and also, as well as
贡献	貢獻	gòngxiàn	V/N to contribute; contribution (in abstract sense)
激动	激動	jīdòng	V/ADJ to get excited; excited
感觉	感覺	gǎnjué	V/N to feel, sense (that); feeling
原谅	原諒	yuánliàng	V to forgive
首先		shǒuxiān	MA first of all, firstly
感谢	感謝	gǎnxiè	V/N to thank, be grateful for; thank, appreciation
领导	領導	lǐngdǎo	V/N to lead; leader; leadership

人员。在我们的学习期间，你们为我们花了很多时间和心血，帮助我们学习汉语和中国文化。我们今天的进步和成绩是和你们的努力分不开的。我们也要感谢你们对我们生活上的关心，使我们在这里生活得很愉快。其次，我们很高兴在学习期间认识了很多中国学生，跟他们的交流使我们有机会在课外和日常生活中了解中国文化和生活。在中国的这段时间里，我们学到了很多东西。虽然刚来的时候我们都很不习惯这里的生活方式，有几次真的想回国去了。我记得有一次玛丽躲在宿舍里哭，雅克也说过要买飞机票回巴黎 了。可是我们慢慢地都适应了，也越来越喜欢这里的一切。现在要离开了，我们还真有点舍不得。总之：我们喜欢中国，喜欢中国文化，也喜欢中国人。我的话说完了。谢谢大家！

张老师：好，大为讲得真好！现在我们进行下一项：发证书。

......

雅克：大为，外面有人找[ii]你。是个漂亮的女孩子，是不是你的女朋友啊？
大为：别开玩笑了！你什么时候看见我有个女朋友？
雅克：那她是谁啊？你快去看看。......
海琳：大为！！没想到[iii]吧？
大为：是你啊！—海琳！！......

ii. “外面有人找你” ("There's someone outside who wants to see you.") 找 is frequently used in spoken Chinese to mean "talk to someone" or "see someone" for a certain purpose. It may not directly relate to the sense of "searching". Examples:
如果你有问题要问，可以找他。（It is awkward to say: 看他 or 跟他说话）
If you have questions [to ask], you may go see (or talk to) him.
昨天我去找他，可是他不在家。I went to see him yesterday, but he was out.

心血		xīnxiě/xīnxuè	N effort, hardwork ("mind and blood")
成绩	成績	chéngjī	N achievement, accomplishment, grade average
其次		qícì	MA secondly
躲		duǒ	V to hide (oneself), avoid (being seen by)
记得	記得	jìde	V to remember
哭		kū	V to cry
巴黎		Bālí	PW Paris
舍不得	捨不得	shěbude	RV to hate to part with, reluctant to let go
总之	總之	zǒngzhī	PH "to sum up", "in conclusion"
发	發	fā	V to issue
证书	證書	zhèngshū	N certificate
没想到		méi xiǎng dào	IE surprisingly, to sb.'s surprise; unexpectedly

回答问题：
1.学校为什么开欢送会？
2.在欢送会上谁代表学校方面讲话？讲了些什么？
3.大为代表谁讲话？他讲了哪几个方面？
4.大为的讲话中哪些话听起来不像美国人的说话方式？
5.大为对海琳的到来感到惊奇吗？

iii. "没想到吧" here means "A surprise [to you], isn't it?" 没想到 (also 想不到) is often used as a phrase by its own or adverbial phrase indicating the speaker's feeling about an unexpected event or discovery, e.g.:

真没想到，他中文说得那么流利！To my surprise, his Chinese is so fluent!
"他考上北京大学了！" "真的？真没想到！" "He is accepted by Beijing University!" "He is? I can't believe it!"
他去年刚结婚，想不到今年就离婚了。He just got married last year, I'm surprised that he has already gotten a divorce this year.

语言结构

Focusing on Structure

Verb-dào For Non-Locomotive Verbs (II)

到 can be compounded with non-locomotive verbs such as学、看、找、猜、了解etc. to convey a sense of "achieving" the purpose or result of the action due to the accessibility or availability of the object. The action verbs of this type are typically goal- or purpose-oriented, suggesting "try to obtain something" such as 找 (to search), 买 (to buy), 看 (to see), 吃 (to eat), 问 (to inquire), and 了解 (to get information about). (到 in this usage is similar to 着 (-zháo) used as a resultative verb ending.)

Examples:

我从这本书上学到了很多东西。	I have learned a lot from this book.
我找来找去还是找不到那本书。	I searched everywhere but still couldn't find the book.
这本书现在买不到。	This book is not sold in stores now. (You can't get this book in stores now.)
你问没问到他的地址？	Have you obtained his address (from your inquiry)?
在中国也看得到美国电影。	You can also see American movies in China.
在中国吃得到吃不到"热狗"？	Are hot dogs sold in China? (Can one get hot dogs in China?)
从他的谈话中我了解到很多中国的情况。	From his conversation I learned a lot about China.

Compare this usage with the one discussed in Lesson 11, in which Verb-到 sentences denote unintentional actions and results, and where 到 cannot be replaced with 着.
Here are some examples:

我今天听到一件奇怪的事。	I heard a strange story today.
我没注意到他穿着什么衣服。	I didn't notice what he wore.

词汇用法
Word Usage

Verbs

- 结束：我去年结束了大学生活。/学习结束了。/结束得很早；晚会很快就结束了。
- 完成：完成学习(学业、工作、一本书...)；早一点完成；什么时候能完成这个工作？/工作完成得很好。
- 鼓励：鼓励学生学中文；鼓励一下；多多鼓励；他给了我很多(很大的)鼓励(N)。
- 继续：继续努力(学习、做、说、讨论、合作、进行...)；我们明天再继续做。
- 促进：促进文化交流(中美关系、经济发展...)；对中美文化交流有很大的促进(N)
- 感谢：非常感谢你的帮忙(照顾、好意...)；我很感谢你帮了我很多忙。
- 花：花时间(心血、钱...)；花两个钟头做家务事；钱花得很多(很随便)
- 躲：躲雨；躲屋子里；你怎么老躲着我？/他来了，我们快躲起来！
- 原谅：原谅你的错；请你原谅我没来上课。/他不原谅我。
- 记得：我不记得他的名字（他的电话号码）。/我记得你说过你喜欢这本书。
- 舍得：你舍得花这么多钱买那个礼物吗？/我舍不得离开这里(丢这本书)。
- 进步：你学习(工作、中文...)进步了；进步得很快；有很大的进步(N)
- 发：发证书（薪水）；学校发给我一张毕业证书。/这个月的薪水月底才发。
- 哭：她哭了。/她动不动就哭。/她哭得很伤心。/哭得眼睛都红了；别哭了。

Verb-Object Compounds

- 开会：开欢送会(舞会、生日晚会、庆祝会...)；开了两个钟头的会；今天的会开得很顺利。
- 讲话：代表学生（学校、公司）讲话；请你给我们讲几句话。/他讲了三分钟的话。/他讲话讲得很短。/他的讲话很有意思。(N)

Resultative Compounds

- V-到：这本书我总算找到了。/我问了好几个人才问到他的电话号码。/哪里可以买到中国食品？/我在这里看不到中国的电视，也吃不到中国菜。/从他那里我没了解到什么情况。/我查到这个人的名字和地址了。

Nouns

- 贡献：为(国家、社会、文化交流...)做出贡献；他的贡献很大（很多）。
- 领导：他是公司的领导。/国家领导人；他领导这个公司(V)。
- 成绩：学习(工作...)成绩；成绩很好(很大)；我的工作很有成绩(Adj)。

句型和习惯用语
Sentence Patterns and Expressions

1.首先……，其次……(**First,…… second,……**) **[formal style]**

- 首先，我要感谢老师给我的帮助和鼓励。其次，我要感谢同学对我的关心。
- 今天的欢送会分三段进行：首先是中心负责人讲话，其次是学生代表讲话，最后是发毕业证书。
- 我公司特别向您推荐这种新产品。这种产品有很多吸引人的特点：首先______________，其次______________。

2.总之，……(**To sum up……; In short,……**) **[formal style]**

- ……总之，我们喜欢中国，喜欢中国文化，也喜欢中国人。
- 他又不能干又不努力又不负责。总之，我们不能继续雇用他。
- She wants a daughter-in-law who is smart, beautiful, capable and is good at housekeeping. In a word, she wants a perfect person.

3.没想到/想不到 **(To sb's surprise,…/ I'm surprised that…)**

- 真没想到，你中文说得这么流利！
  I'm really surprised. You speak Chinese so fluently!
- 我以为中国少数民族不多，想不到有五十多个！
- 他从楼上跳下来，______________________________！
- He and I met just once ten years ago. I was amazed that he still remembered my name after all these years!

文化介绍

Learning About Culture

正式场合中的自谦语

The Convention of Modesty in Formal Language

In previous lessons we have seen that the Chinese, more so than Americans, use conventional language, often in the form of stock phrases, in formal writing, as well as in formal speeches. Even in a simple situation in which one is praised, conventional language is called for. One should not respond to a compliment with a "Thank you." The compliment should be politely deflected by saying, "I don't deserve it," or "I am unworthy of your compliments," or "I have much to learn."

When acknowledging their own achievements, such as the publication of a book, or winning a prize in a contest, Chinese tend to attribute their success to their leaders and colleagues rather than to themselves or their own family members. They are also expected to show modesty by including such phrases as "due to my own limitations and insufficient time, there must be many errors in my work. I'd like to invite your criticism and corrections." Or "Although I have won, I'm still far from your expectations. I need to make further effort...."

The following phrases are commonly used in speech for expressing acknowledgement or gratitude:

- 我的成果是和大家的帮助、鼓励分不开的。
- 我做得还不够，还差得远。
- 我还有很多不足之处(inadequacies)，需要继续学习和努力。
- 我应该向大家学习。
- 希望大家多多指教。

第十八课听力练习

第一部分：单句

请你们听下面的句子。每个句子的意思是什么？请在三个选择中选出一句来。

1. (a)我读了这本书以后，对中国文化方面的事有了更多的了解。
   (b)我从这本书里学不到什么东西。
   (c)阅读这本书对我没有帮助。

2. (a)我们猜他会躲在浴室里，可是猜得不对。
   (b)我们在浴室里找到他。
   (c)我们没猜着他会躲在浴室里。

3. (a)你想象得到他的成绩有多好吗？
   (b)你是否注意到他的成绩比以前进步了？
   (c)你关心不关心他的成绩怎么样？

4. (a)我是第一次到昆明旅游。
   (b)到昆明旅游是我毕业后想做的第一件事。
   (c)我毕业后想先做事，然后再到昆明旅游。

5. (a)只要常听录音、常看中文书，你就能把汉语学好。
   (b)想要学好汉语，你最少得做到三件事：第一，要有好老师；第二要有好书；第三，你得常常跟着录音带练习。
   (c)有了好老师和好书，你就能把汉语学好。

6. (a)我们总算知道我们的领导是一个什么样的人了。
   (b)他总是喜欢找认真负责、有经验、有学问的人当领导。
   (c)能力、责任心、经验、学问和想法，他什么都有，当我们的领导再合适不过了。

第二部分：对话

对话一:请把这个对话听两遍，然后看看下面的句子说得对不对。

_____1.这两个人刚从大学毕业。

_____2.毕业了，这两个人都觉得很开心。

_____3.老师在欢送会上所讲的话，使第一个人很激动。

_____4.第二个人希望越早离开学校越好。

对话二:

第一遍:请你们听懂这个对话的大意，然后看看下面的句子说得对不对。

_____1.小杨在给她美国的老师写信。

_____2.小杨很感谢她的美国朋友给了她很多帮忙和照顾。

_____3.小杨跟她那位美国朋友是在一个晚会中认识的。

_____4.小杨跟她的美国朋友兴趣不一样。

第二遍:请你们读下面的问题，然后把这个对话再听一次。听完后，请回答问题。

1.小杨为什么要写信感谢她的美国朋友？

2.小杨是怎么认识那位美国朋友的？

3.小杨从跟她的美国朋友相处中学到了什么？

第十八课 练习
词汇；句型；语法

I.填空：

1.结束：电影________？/________在中国的学习。/我们的参观明天就________。

2.鼓励：他鼓励我________。/我很感谢你________我的鼓励。/在学中文方面我受____他______的鼓励。/他给了我很______鼓励。

3.促进：我们这样做是为了促进________。/这样做______中国的经济会有________。

4.贡献：他____公司的发展很有______。/他的贡献很______。/他______我们两国的贸易交流______过贡献。

5.原谅：我已经______他好几次了。/这件事我错了，希望能______你的原谅。

6.进步：你的______进步了。/他进步得______。/他自从努力学习后就______了很多。/他的工作很________。

7.成绩：你的工作很______。/他的______成绩______。

8.继续：我已经大学毕业了，可是我想________。/你不必继续____下去了，他们不想听了。

9.交流：我们鼓励两国在________的交流。/我们的交流很______。/我跟他常常交流________。/关于这个问题我曾经跟他________好几次。

II.用适当的"V-到"形式填空：（看-、见-、听-、了解-、找-、买-、学-）

1.这本书很有用，你可以＿＿＿＿＿＿很多商业术语。

2.从跟外商的交流中，我们＿＿＿＿一些关于美国经济发展方面的情况。

3.你们在中国＿＿＿＿＿＿＿美国电影吗？

4.去年我去中国的时候，没有＿＿＿＿＿＿我的老同学，因为他出国了。

5.这本书很难买，我去了好几个书店都＿＿＿＿＿＿＿。

6.我忘了我把他的地址和电话号码放在哪儿了，怎么找也＿＿＿＿＿＿。

7.自从他离开台湾以后，我一直＿＿＿＿＿＿＿＿＿＿他的消息。

阅读练习

感谢信

xx大学中文系：

今年春季我公司开办秘书培训班，贵系派出两位老师为我们开设了古代汉语、语法、公函写作等课程。两位老师讲课认真、生动有趣，课后热心为学员们做辅导。经过几个月的学习，学员们都感到进步很大，在结业考试中取得了好成绩。

两位老师对工作热情、负责的精神，给我们所有的学员留下了深刻的印象。我们从他们那里不但学到了知识，也学到了好作风。

现在我们的培训结束了，我们对两位老师几个月来对我们的辛勤教诲表示深深的感谢。我们要用今后的工作成绩来报答老师对我们的关心和帮助。

特向贵系致以谢意！

云兴公司秘书培训班全体学员

1994年4月30日

回答问题：

1.是什么人写的这封感谢信？信是写给谁的？

2.信里感谢的是谁？为什么事情？

3.信是在什么时候写的？为什么这个时候写？

4.信里的哪些词汇是书面语的词汇？口语里怎么说？

明信片

POST CARD

张老师：

你好！你猜猜我现在是在哪里？我在敦煌！谢谢你推荐我到中国来学习，我在这里过得很快乐。我现在放暑假，所以和几个同学一起到敦煌来了。因为我学的是美术，所以看看敦煌的壁画对我很有用。我们打算下一次到西藏去旅游，也想去昆明看看，听说那里气候四季如春，所以寒假去最好。你怎么样？还在哥大教中文吧？希望你一切都好。我大概在十二月底回美。

你的学生 Patti

Phyllis Zhang
Kent Hall
room 414
Columbia Univeisity
116th Broadway
New York. N.Y. 10025
USA

[illegible]像群（唐代）
Group of Painted Clay Figures (Tang Dynasty)

回答问题：

1.这张明信片是什么人写的？写给谁的？

2.写信者现在在哪里？为什么？

3.写信者有什么打算？

口语练习

I.回答下面的问题：

1. 什么样的会叫做“欢送会”？开欢送会的时候大家做些什么？
2. 什么情况下一个人会激动？人激动的时候会有什么样的感觉和表现？
3. “做贡献”这个词是什么意思？请举例说明。
4. 在中国，感谢信常常是写给一个单位而不是给朋友的。而且是用一张很大的红纸写，贴在外面好让大家都能看到。在你的文化里，什么情况下应该写感谢信？用什么样的语言写（正式、半正式、口语）？

II.发言/讲话练习：

你在一个中国学校学习了一段时间，现在学习结束了，在欢送会上想讲几句话，表达自己的感谢。你怎么讲？

常用语

我的成绩是和＿＿＿＿＿＿＿＿给我的帮助分不开的。

感谢＿＿＿＿＿＿＿＿这一年来给我的鼓励。

我的＿＿＿＿＿＿还不够好（还差得很远），我还要继续努力。

我也要感谢＿＿＿＿＿＿＿对我生活上的关心和照顾。

我希望今后能＿＿＿＿＿＿＿＿＿＿＿＿＿＿＿。

写作练习

1.写感谢信：你的学习结束了，你和同学们要写一封感谢信给学校的有关领导和老师。

2.写明信片：练习写一张明信片给你的中国朋友。(请把地址写在右边。)

附录
APPENDICES

A. 句型和习惯用语
Sentence Patterns and Expressions Index

B. 词汇表
Vocabulary Glossary

Appendix A
句型和习惯用语(1-18课)
Sentence Patterns and Expressions Index (Lessons 1-18)

Note: This list goes by the alphabetical order of the first character. In the rare occasion when no character is found in the pattern or expression, alphabetical order of the first English word is followed. Lesson number is listed at the end of each pattern/expression.

按(照)...的V法，...... (According to ..., ...) 10

按照他的说法，电脑并不难学。 According to his view, a computer is not hard to learn.

.....按......V ([Sb.] does sth. according to...) 10

他从来不按规定做事。 He never does things according to the rules

把 A Verb成 B... (take sth. for another; make sth. into another) 14

哎呀！你把酱油放成醋了！ Oh no! You added vinegar instead of soysauce!

把 A叫作 B (call A "B") 10

我们把这个节日叫作春节。 We call this holiday the "Spring Festival."

包括......(在内)，......(Including..., ... [totals] ...; include ....) 7

包括我在内，这里一共有二十六个人。Including me, there are twenty-six people here.

明天的考试包括这一课的生字（在内）。Tomorrow's test will cover the new words of this lesson.

别看......其实......(Don't be fooled/misled by [the fact that...] Actually......) 14

别看她很少念书，其实她的功课非常好。

Don't be misled by her not studying much. Actually, she does very well on her school work.

不但 ......,而且（也）......(not only ... but also...) 4

他不但（不）熟悉美国的情况，而且也（不）熟悉中国的情况

He is not only familiar with the goings-on in the U.S., but also with those in China.

不管......，都 V......(no matter what/who/when/where/how...) 3

不管我说什么，他都不听。No matter what I say, he just won't listen.

不是A,就是B (It is either A or B; If it's not A, it must be B) 6

大为的电话真不好打，不是占线，就是没人接。

Itüs hard to reach David by phone. Either the line is busy or no one answers the phone.

(.......)不是......吗？(Rhetorical: Isn't it the case that...?) 13

西方不是也有龙的神话吗？ The West also has myths about dragons, doesn't it?

(Clause) +（不要紧/很重要/很好/不好）(It is [unimportant / important /good/bad,etc.] to/ that...) 5

学得慢不要紧，可是一定要努力。

It's OK if you are slow (in studying), but you must study hard.

房间够不够大很重要。Whether the room is large enough is very important.

晚上一个人在街上走不好。Itüs not good to walk by oneself in the street late at night.

不知道......怎么样？(I wonder what...is like?) 7

不知道这里的环境怎么样？I wonder what the environment here is like.

不知道怎么搞的，......(who knows how it happened...; I've no idea ...; somehow...) 4

不知道怎么搞的，我这几天总是睡不好觉。I don't know why these days I haven't been sleeping well.

曾经V过 (ever did sth. in the past) 9

我曾经在中国待过一段时间。 I once stayed in China for a period of time.

趁......V (taking advantage of... to do...) 6

趁我父母不在家，我赶快给他打了个电话。

Taking advantage of my parents' not being home, I hurriedly gave him a call.

趁早V (do sth. as early as possible / while one can / before it's too late) 6

如果你不爱他，就趁早跟他吹了吧。

If you don't love him, why don't you break up with him before it's too late.

V出O来;V出来+clause (Sb. detects ... through doing...) 12

我听出他的意思来了。 I figured out (from what he said) what he really meant.

除非......否则......(unless..., otherwise...) 17

除非您的订货量大，否则我们一般是不给折扣的。

Generally we don't give discounts unless you place a large order.

除了......以外，也/还......(Besides/except..., sb./sth. also....) 10

除了他以外，我也是中国人。Besides him, I'm also Chinese.

除了他以外，我们都是中国人。Except him, we are all Chinese.

从......中（看出来，了解到，发现，...）(From ... [sb.] discover\learn about\ find, etc.) 15

从学校布告栏的启事中可以了解到学生们在想些什么，做些什么。

You can learn about what students are thinking and doing from the notices on the school bulletin board.

......,从中V....(..., from which, sb. [know,discover,etc.]....) 15

我常常看中文报纸，从中可以了解很多中国的情况。

I often read Chinese newspapers, from which I can learn about things in China.

当A还在......时，B已经......了 (When A is/was still..., B already...) 16

当北京还在下大雪时，昆明已经开满鲜花了。

When it is still snowing in Beijing, flowers are already in full bloom all over Kunming.

到底 (what/who/when/where/how in the world......?) 2

这到底是怎么回事？ What exactly is going on?

他到底是谁？ Who on earth is he?/ Who exactly is he?

V1的V1，V2的V2 (some are doing/did..., others are doing/did...) 11

他家里很热闹，聊天的聊天，包饺子的包饺子。

Itüs very festive in his house: some people are chatting while others are making dumplings.

Adj. / V 得...... (Sb. / sth. ... so ...that...) 1

我高兴得说不出话来。 I was so happy that I was speechless.

(Clause), V/Adj. 得 sb.(+ result/extent)(...so much so that it causes/caused...) 5

他老在宿舍里唱歌，唱得我头大。

He always sings in the dorm and that drives me crazy.

V得成/V不成；V成了/没V成 (can\can't realize a plan; succeeded/failed in realizing/fulfilling...) 14

我们最好早点儿买票，要不然可能就看不成那个电影了。

We'd better buy the tickets early, otherwise we might not be able to see the movie.

......得......才行 (Sb. has got to do ...before...) 4

你得适应这里的条件才行。You've got to get adjusted to the conditions here.

等......再V......(wait until ... and then...) 6

等我把功课复习完了再跟你出去看电影。

After I finish reviewing my lessons, I'll go to the movies with you.

动不动就V ..... (VP at every possible moment; easily......) [negative connotation] 12

你怎么动不动就生气？How come you got mad over nothing?!

都怪...... (It's all sb's fault that...; Sb. is to blame) 8

你一喝酒就醉，都怪你不会克制自己。You get drunk every time you drink and you are the one to blame because you don't know how to control yourself.

对......感/有兴趣 (be interested in...; to take interest in....) 9

我对这个工作很感兴趣。 I am very interested in this job.

对......来说，......(As far as Sb. is concerned...; For Sb. ...) 1

这一次分别，对他们两个人来说都有一点儿不容易。

It is not easy at all for the two of them to part this time.

多Verb (quantity).... ([do] more...) 17

今天的人很多，你多做一点菜。 We have many people here today, please make more food.

.....,而 ....却..... ([Clause], whereas/however ...) 14

四川菜比较辣，而广东菜却比较温和。

Sichuanese cuisine tends to be spicy, whereas Cantonese cuisine is comparatively mild.

...非（要）......不可 (Sb. must do...\ Sb. insists on...) 12

如果想说好中文，你非每天练习不可。

If you want to be fluent in Chinese, you must practice every day.

今天天气不好，可他非要今天去不可。

The weather is bad today, but he insists on going there today.

该V了（It's time to......） 3

你已经三十多岁了，该结婚了。

You're already over thirty. It's time for you to get married!

A跟B很相似（A and B are very much alike / A is similar to B） 13

龙的形象跟闪电很相似。 The shape of the dragon is similar to that of lightning.

A跟B有关（A [effect/result] has something to do with B [cause/source]...） 10

这件事一定跟他有关。 This must have something to do with him.

关于......的 (N.) (regarding.../concerning.../about...) 17

想谈谈关于出国留学方面的事情/问题。 I'd like to talk about studying abroad.

....,还是......的好。(I think [upon reflection] that it is better for me [you, him, etc.] to do...) 17

今天雪太大，我们还是不出去的好。The snowfall is heavy today. Maybe it's better that we stay home.

好(不)容易才V (had great difficulty before finally...) 8

我找了几个月，好(不)容易才找到一个满意的公寓。

I looked for an apartment for months [and had a hard time] before I finally found a satisfactory one.

.....,好让......(Sb. did sth. in order for sb. to ...\ ... so that sb. could ...) 16

我把大门打开，好让客人把车子开进来。I opened the gate, so that the guest could drive in.

……，好在……（..., fortunately, ...） 5

我前几天忙死了，好在他来了，帮了我不少忙。

I was extremely busy a few days ago. Fortunately he came and helped me a great deal.

何必……(呢)？（Rhetorical: why bother about...? \ why should\must...?） 12

他是开玩笑的，你何必认真？He is just joking, why do you have to take it personally?

既……又……(...both... and ...) 既不（没）...又不（没）...(neither...nor...) 15

他既有能力又有经验。He is both capable and experienced. (He has both ability and experience.)

他既没有能力又没有经验。He has neither ability nor experience.

既然……，那（么）……(Since [that is the case], then....) 10

既然她要给你介绍对象，那就让她介绍吧。

Since she wants to introduce to you a potential mate; why don't you just let her.

……，加上……，结果……（..., plus... then,[sth. happened]) 5

他到了新地方，身体不适应，加上又喜欢吃生冷的东西，结果生了一 次病。

He had just come to a new place and wasn't accustomed to the new environment. Moreover, he likes to eat raw or cold food; then, he got sick.

……将于……V(Sb. will do...\Sth. will be done [at time\place]) 15

我校将于下个月开始招生。Our school will begin to enroll new students next month.

借...机会V（take the opportunity to ...） 3

他想借留学中国的机会好好地熟悉一下中国的情况。

He wants to take the opportunity of studying abroad in China to get familiar with China.

Sb. ...(QW-form) 就...(QW-form) （sb. does whatever sb. wants to ...） 8

谁想吃什么就吃什么吧。 Anyone can eat whatever he/she wants.

就V好了（Why don't you just......） 8

我叫李大为，你就叫我大为好了。My name is Li Dawei. Why don't you just call me Dawei.

A就是B的意思（A means/refers to B） 10

"亲友"就是亲戚和朋友的意思。"亲友" means "relatives and friends."

(Location)就是 (Place) (Right at [location] is [place] / You'll find [place] right at [location]） 7

学校前头就是一条大马路。A broad street is right in fornt of the school.

街对面就是银行。The bank is right across the street.

就是……，也……（even if..., sb/sth....） 4
你就是给他钱，他也不会愿意做这件事的。He won't do this even if you give him money.

据...所Verb，...（According to....../based on what is said, reported, etc. [from source]） 13
据我所知，他是学经济的。 As far as I know, he is an economics major.

看上去......(...looks/looked like...) 7
她看上去只有五十多岁。 She looks like she is only in her fifties.

看样子......(It seems/looks like...) 2
看样子他不会来了。 It doesn't look like he is coming./It looks like he is not coming.

V来V去，就是 (neg.)...（Sb. kept doing sth. but just couldn't / didn't...） 2
我想来想去，就是想不出一个好法子来。
I thought about it over and over, but I just couldn't come up with a good idea.

VP了 (+ comment)（If/Once sb. [does/has done...], then [sth. will happen]） 5
你得早一点到食堂去，去晚了就买不到饭了。
You'd better go to the cafeteria earlier. If you go there late you won't be able to buy food.

(连)...都...，更别说...了（even......, let alone......） 12
快考试了，我聊天的时间都没有，更别说跟你出去玩了！
I have an exam coming up. I don't even have the time to chat, let alone hanging out with you!

Location/Time + Locomotive Verb + indef. performer (indef. Performer + Locomotive Verb + [Location/Time]) 2
前面走过来几个人。 A few people were approaching from the distance ahead.

麻烦你V...。/麻烦你V......好吗？(Please [do me a favor and].../ Could you please [do...]?) 6
麻烦你请他接一下电话好吗？Could you tell him to answer the phone please?

忙着......(sb.is/was busy doing... [during/when...]) 7
这几天她正在忙着找房子。She is busy looking for a house these days.

没(duration of time)就V了（sb.\ sth. .... in less than [time]） 4
他到了美国以后，没两天就生病了。 He got sick just a few days after he arrived in the U.S.

没想到/想不到 (To sb's surprise,.../ I'm surprised that...) 18
真没想到，你中文说得这么流利！ I'm really surprised: you speak Chinese so fluently!

(Sb.\Sth.)哪(里)...... ? (Rhetorical: How can it be the case that...?) 12

她每天都那么忙，哪(里)有时间照顾家庭？

She is so busy every day. How does she manage to find the time to take care of her family?

这本书哪里是他的？How can this book be his?

你看(说、觉得)(Sb.) V...好？(What would you suggest?/What [where, etc.] do you think [sb.] should ...?) 8

我想买一点儿吃的东西，你看（我）买什么好？I'd like to buy some food. What do you think/suggest/recommend I should buy?

.....你看(说，觉得，认为)怎么样？(......What do you think?) 9

我们今天晚上出去吃饭，你看怎么样？Let's eat out tonight. What do you think?

.....，其中...... (......, among whom/which; of which ...) 2

我有二十本书，其中有五本中文书。 I have twenty books, five of which are Chinese books.

...V-起来... (Sb. / Sth. is ... when ...; Sth. is ... to [do]) 11

他看起来不像中国人。He doesn't look like a Chinese.

他做起事来很认真。He is serious when doing his job.

千万(别)...... (Do/Don't do......by all/any means!) 11

自己一个人到国外去，千万要特别小心。Do be specially careful when going abroad by yourself.

他是开玩笑的，你千万别生气。He was just joking. Do not get angry, please!

...... 使 ...... (Sb. / Sth. makes / made sb. / sth. ....) 7

他的话使我很高兴。 His words made me happy./His words pleased me.

Sb.是第一次...... (It is sb's first time......) 2

你是第一次来纽约吗？ Is this your first time in New York?

是否......(Is it...or not? Do/Does ...or not?) [formal style] 17

你是否参观过那个博物馆？ Have you ever visited that museum?

不知道那种产品的质量是否可靠？ I wonder whether the quality of that product is reliable or not.

受...；受到...（欢迎，重视，喜爱...）(...received [popularity, attention, favor, etc.]) 8

这个饭馆受到很多顾客欢迎。 /这个饭馆很受顾客欢迎。

This restaurant is favored by many customers.

首先……，其次……(First,…… second,……) [formal style] 18

首先，我要感谢老师给我的帮助和鼓励。其次，我要感谢同学对我的关心。

First of all, I'd like to thank my teachers for their encouragement. Secondly, I also wish to thank the Chinese students for their help.

虽然……，但是总比……多了 (Although...yet it's much more... than...) 5

虽然这个房子不够大，可是总比宿舍好多了。

Although this house is not big enough, it is much better than the dormitory.

万万…；万万别…；万万没想到…(... under no circumstances/ by no means) 12

你万万不能做这件事！ Under no circumstances should you do this!

我万万没想到他会被那个公司雇用。I had never ever imagined he'd be hired by that company.

(building, city...)位于……(... is located at...) [formal style] 16

电脑中心位于图书馆的左边。The Computer Lab is located to the left of the library.

Subject 为 (sb. / sth)……（而）… (Subject is / does... for the sake of/because of/on behalf of ...) 3

他一天到晚为家事而忙得团团转。

Because of his housework, he is always so busy that he doesnüt know he is coming or going.

为了……，…… (in order to; for the sake of) 1

为了把中文说好，大为要到北京去学习。

David will go to Beijing to study in order to speak Chinese well.

我以为……哪知道…… (I had thought/had assumed..., but I was surprised to find that...) 12

我以为他什么都不懂，哪知道他其实很有学问。

I thought he was quite ignorant, but to my surprise, he is actually very knowledgeable.

无(monosyllabic noun)不(monosyllabic verb) (There is no...that sb.\sth. not V...) 13

这个人无事不做。There is nothing this man doesn't do. (He does all kinds of things.)

无所不(monosyllabic verb) (There is nothing that sb.\sth...does not V) 13

我跟她无所不谈。

There is nothing that she and I cannot talk about. (We talk about everything.)

像.....这样/那样(.....)的(N.)(sb./sth [so.....] like .....) 12

像他那样的人，对你再合适不过了。A man like him is just the best guy for you.

我想住在像纽约那样热闹的地方。I want to live in a place as lively and busy as New York.

要不是（因为）(reality) ......，还.....（呢）\就 (counter-reality)......了 (But for the fact..., sb. would \would have done...) 16

要不是因为该回北京上课了，大为还真不想离开这个美丽的城市（呢）。

If it had not been time to go back to Beijing for classes, David wouldn't have left this pretty city yet.

一边 ......，一边 ...... (Sb. does/did one thing while doing another) 5

他一边看书，一边听流行歌曲。He listened to hit/popular songs while reading.

一是 ......，二是 ...... (for one thing..., for another...) 3

我没有去找他，一是我太忙，二是我不知道他住在哪里。

I didnüt go to see him, because for one I was too busy, and for another, I didnüt know where he lives.

.....以 ......为主 (...consists mainly of...) 10

年画的颜色以红色为主。The primary color used on Chinese New Year's posters is red.

...以 ......闻名 (sth.\ sb.is famous for...) [formal style] 16

昆明以气候温和闻名。 Kunming is famous for its mild climate.

应该 ......才 ...... (It's only [good,right,etc.]...for sb. to...) 11

他说："你应该说 '哪里哪里'才像中国话。"

He said: "You should say 'Not really,' and then it would sound more like Chinese."

应邀到 ...来/去 V (come / go to...to do sth....upon invitation) 11

大为应邀到刘东家去做客。 Upon invitation, David went to Liu Dong's house as a guest.

由 A 经 B 到 C (from A via B to C) [formal/written style] 16

他们由南京经成都最后到了昆明。

From Nanjing they passed through Chengdu and finally arrived in Kunming.

.....，于是 (sb.) 就 V 了 ...... (..., so/thereupon sb. did sth. [as an immediate reaction]) 9

那个电脑很好用，而且也不贵，于是我就买了。

That computer is user-friendly and it's not expensive either, so I bought it.

在 ......上 (in terms of...; in the area of...; -wise) 11

中国人在社交上有些什么规矩？ What norms do the Chinese people have in terms of socializing?

...再...也没有了/不过了 (Sth. couldn't be better / worse, etc. ...) 3

这个人又聪明，长得又帅，对你再合适也没有了。

This man is both smart and handsome. He is the perfect one for you/No one could be more suitable.

再过 time expression，就 V. ...了 (Sb./sth. will [...] in + [time]) 1

再过几天就是我妹妹的生日了。It will be my younger sister's birthday in a few days.

.....，再说...也，......所以......(.... Besides,..., so......) 12

他没有这方面的工作经验，再说，他也不会用电脑，所以我们不能雇用他 He is not experienced in this area. Besides, he doesn't know how to use the computer either, so we can't hire him.

早不......晚不......，偏偏在...的时候V (Sb. does/did sth. at the worst time) 4

他早不来晚不来，偏偏在我要睡觉了的时候来了！(真要命！) He didn't come at a good time but chose to come just when I was about to go to sleep! Damn it!

Location +V 着+ sb./ sth. (There at [place] [verb] sth./sb.) 2

门上贴着一张字条。 On the door is attached a note.

Verb着... (... by means of...; when done by way of...) 14

有的菜煮着好吃，有的菜炒着好吃。

Some foods are tastier when stewed; others are tastier when stir-fried.

V1 着V2 (Sb. is/has ....[accompaniment or means] while doing sth.) 4

他喜欢开着窗户睡觉。He likes to sleep with the window open.

你别看着报纸吃饭。Do not eat your meal and read papers at the same time.

V 着V 着,V/Adj.起(O)来 (While..., ...started to ...) 4

这几天我老咳嗽。咳着咳着，头也疼起来了。

These few days I've coughed all the time. As I coughed, my head began to hurt.

......，这说明......(it indicates that...; it tells you that...) 11

中国人说“礼多人不怪”，这说明中国人很重视礼貌。

Chinese people say "You won't be blamed for being too polite." That indicates that Chinese people do value courtesy.

用......来.....(... use sth. to do sth. /serve the purpose of...) 13

很多部落都用动物来做部落的象征。

Many tribes used animal images to serve as their tribal emblems.

(time expression)(以)来...... (during/over the past [days/months,etc.],...) 1

这一个月(以)来，我看了不少书。 I have read quite a few books during the past month.

这(time expression)(以)来， Sb.都在V... (Sb. has been doing sth. for the past...) 1

这一个月来，他都在作出国准备。

He has been making preparations for going abroad for the past month.

.....，这就是...的缘故 (..., and that is the reason why...) 13

他昨天病了，这就是他(为什么)没有来的缘故。 He was sick yesterday. That's why he didn't come.

只要......（就）......(as long as..., then...; ... provided that...) 7

只要你有钱，你就可以住很漂亮的房子。

You can live in a beautiful house as long as you have money.

...主要是......(mainly...; primarily...) 9

我们公司想找的业务代表主要是用英文。

The sales representative that our company is looking for will primarily speak and write in English.

自从......(point of time)以后，就... ...了(Ever since..., ...) 6

他自从结婚以后，就没再给我打过电话了。 He hasn't called me since he got married.

A 总比 B Adj. 多了 (A is at least much more [adj.] than B.) 4

打电话总比写信快多了。Making a phone call is at least much faster than writing a letter.

左V右V，都(neg.)....../总算 (pos.)......了(kept doing sth, but still.../and finally...) 6

我左盼右盼都盼不来他的信。I kept hoping to get letters from him, but I just never got any.

我左等右等都等不到他的电话。/我左等右等，总算等到了他的电话了。

I waited and waited; his phone call finally came.

Appendix B
词汇表(1-18课)
Vocabulary Glossary (Lessons 1 - 18)

A:

ài shàng	爱上/愛上	RV to fall in love with 5
àn	按	V to press; push down, depress 6
àn	按	CV according to 7
ānjìng	安靜/安静	ADJ quiet (安安静静地,quietly) 5
ānpái	安排	V/N to arrange, schedule; arrangement 3
ānquán	安全	ADJ safe, secure 7
ànshí	按时/按時	CV-O on time, [do...] according to scheduled time 7
ànzhào	按照	CV according to 10

B:

bǎi	摆/擺	V to display; arrange 12
bài//nián	拜年	VO to pay New Year's tributes 10
Bālí	巴黎	PW Paris 18
bàng	棒	ADJ [slang] super, excellent 11
bàngōngshì	办公室/辦公室	N office, workplace (办公, VO to work [in an office]); (-室, -room) 2
bāngzhù	帮助/幫助	V/N to assist, help; assistance 1
bāo	包	V [colloq.] to guarantee (sb. for sth.) 15
bào	抱	V to hold in arms, embrace 12
bǎochí	保持	V to keep (clean, etc.), to maintain 7
bāokuò	包括	V to include, contain 7
bāokuò...zài nèi	包括...在内	VP including, with......included 7
bào//míng	报名/報名	VO to apply, sign up 15
bāozhuāng	包装/包裝	V to pack, packaging 8
bāozi	包子	N steamed stuffed bun (肉包子, bun stuffed with meat) 4
bèi	被	CV (passive voice marker) 10
biānpào	鞭炮	N firecrackers 10
biǎo	表	N chart, table, list, form 9
biǎoyǎn	表演	V/N to give a performance; performance, show 10
bǐfāngshuō	比方说/比方說	PH for example 5
bǐjiào	比较/比較	V/A to compare; comparatively, relatively 14

bǐng	饼/餅	N cake, pie, cookie 8
bìng	病	N/V disease, ailment; to be sick 4
bìngqiě	並且	MA moreover, and, and also (syn. ěrqiě, 而且) 5
bǐrúshuō	比如说/比如說	PH for example, for instance 14
bì(shang)	闭(上)/閉(上)	RV to close (eyes, mouth, etc.) 6
bìyè	毕业/畢業	VO/N to graduate; graduation 3
bō	拨/撥	V to dial (the telephone), set/adjust (a watch, dial, etc.) 6
bómǔ	伯母	N wife of father's elder brother; aunt 3
bóshì	博士	N (academic) doctor 15
bówùguǎn	博物馆/博物館	N museum 13
bù	-部	BF area, region (as PW Suffix) 1
búdàn...érqiě	不但...而且	MA not only..., but also... 4
bùgàolán	布告栏/佈告欄	N bulletin board 15
bùguǎn	不管	MA no matter, regardless 3
bújiànde	不见得/不見得	MA [colloq.] not necessarily 5
bùluò	部落	N tribe 13
(yào)bùrán	(要)不然	MA otherwise 5
bǔxí	补习/補習	V/N to take lessons in order to meet requirements; to give tutoring lessons; supplemental study 15

C:

cānguān	参观/參觀	V/N to tour, visit (a place); tour, visit 13
cānjiā	参加/參加	V to participate, join 8
cāntīng	餐厅/餐廳	N cafeteria; restaurant 15
céngjīng	曾经/曾經	A (did/was) once, ever 9
chá	查	V to check, check over; look up (name, phone number, etc.) 6
chà	差	ADJ poor (in quality, ability) 9
cháng	尝/嚐	V to taste, sample (food) 14
chángtú	长途/長途	N long distance; long distance phone call 6
chǎnpǐn	产品/產品	N product 9
chǎo	炒	V to saute, stir-fry 14
cháodài	朝代	N dynasty 13
chèn	趁	CV take advantage of (a favorable situation) 6
chéng	成	V to turn into, become 1
chéng	乘	CV [formal] by (means of transportation) (syn. of 坐) 16
Chéngdū	成都	PW (name of city in China) 16

chēnghū	称呼/稱呼	V/N to address, call (also:称); form of address 11
chéngjī	成绩/成績	N achievement, accomplishment, grade average 18
chéngshì	城市	N city(shortened as 市 after a name) 16
chéngwéi	成为/成為	EV (after a time) to become (sb./sth.) 13
chéngyǔ	成语/成語	N (usu.) four-character idiom; set phrase 13
chènzǎo	趁早	A (do) while you can 6
chí	池	N pond, small lake 16
chídào	迟到/遲到	V to arrive late (for class, meeting) 5
chīlì	吃力	V/ADJ to make strenuous effort; effort-taking 15
chī yào	吃药/吃藥	VO to take medicine (orally); (药, medicine, remedy) 4
chóngbài	崇拜	V/N to worship, idolize; worship 13
chū	出	V to contribute, chip in (idea, money, etc.) 6
chuántǒng	传统/傳統	N tradition 10
chúfáng	厨房/廚房	N kitchen 7
chúfēi	除非	MA unless 17
chuī le	吹了	IE [colloq.] (relationship) broken up/split; (of a plan) failed/fell through 3
chūjí	初级/初級	N beginner level 15
chūkǒu	出口	V/N to export; export 9
chūkǒuchù	出口处/出口處	N exit (出口 N exit; -处 -place, Noun-Suffix) 2
chúle...yǐwài	除了...以外	CONJ aside from, besides 10
chǔlǐ	处理/處理	V to handle, process, take care of (a matter) 17
Chūnjié	春节/春節	N Chinese New Year ("Spring Festival") 10
chūxiàn	出现/出現	V/N to appear, emerge; appearance, emergence 13
chūzū	出租	V lease out; leased. 2
chūzūchē	出租车/出租車	N taxi ('Taxi' is 计程车/計程車 [jìchéngchē] in Taiwan) 2
cí	词/詞	N word, term 11
cíhuì	词汇/詞彙	N vocabulary, terminology 15
cōng	葱	N scallion 14
cù	醋	N vinegar 14
cùjìn	促进/促進	V to promote (friendship, understanding, etc.) 18
cūn	村	N village 16

D:

dá	打	M a dozen (note tone!) 8
dǎ	打	V to hit, beat 10
dǎ pēntì	打喷嚏/打噴嚏	VO to sneeze 4
dǎ//léi	打雷	VO to thunder 13

dīng	叮	(sound simulation of a phone ring/bell) 6
dàduōshù	大多数/大多數	N/AV/A majority; most (people, etc.) mostly 10
dāi	待	V to stay (at a place or for a time) 3
dài háizi	带孩子/帶孩子	VP to bring up a child,look after a child 12
dàibiǎo	代表	V/N to represent; representative 9
dàimàn	怠慢	V to neglect (a guest, senior, etc.) 11
dàngāo	蛋糕	N layer cake; cake 8
dāngshí	当时/當時	TW at that time, then, at that very moment 1
dāng...yǐhòu	当...以后/當...以後	TW after 13
dàngzuò	当作/當作	EV to treat sb./sth. As 14
dānzi	单子/單子	N list 17
dàochù	到处/到處	PW everywhere 4
dàodǐ	到底	MA after all 2
dàodá	到达/到達	V/N to reach, arrive; arrival 2
dàolǐ	道理	N reason, logic 13
dàolái	到来/到來	V/N to arrive; arrival 10
dàoshì	倒(是)	A actually, on the other hand 8
dǎsǎo	打扫/打掃	V. to clean (by mopping or sweeping) 7
dàzhuān	大专/大專	N university & professional school (abbr. of 大学 and 专科学校 / 專科學校zhuānkē xuéxiào) 9
...dehuà	...的话/...的話	IE if... 11
Diānchí	滇池	PW (name of a lake in Kunming, China) 16
dìdiǎn	地点/地點	N location, place (of an event) 8
dìng	订/訂	V to place an order; make a reservation 17
dìnggòu	订购/訂購	V to order (for purchasing) 17
dìngjīn	定金	N deposit (money paid in advance) 7
dìqū	地区/地區	PW area, region 7
dìzhǐ	地址	N address 5
dòngbudòng jiù...	动不动就.../動不動就...	A (do...) too easily/frequently; always (ready to)... 12
dōngtiān	冬天	N winter 16
dòngwù	动物/動物	N animal 13
Dōngyà	东亚/東亞	PW East Asia 3
dōu	都	A [colloq.] already 12
dòufu	豆腐	N beancurd, tofu 14
dū	嘟	(sound of tone heard on the phone) 6
dú	读/讀	V to read, to study (sth.) 12
dù	度	M degree (of temperature, angle, etc.) 4

duàn	段	M section, part 1
duìfāng	对方/對方	N the other party 6
duì le	对了/對了	IE [colloq.] By the way, ...; Oh yeah, 12
duìlián	对联/對聯	N (poetic) couplets (two-line verses composed in parallel phrases/sen tences) 10
duìxiàng	对象/對象	N (marriage) prospect; target, object 3
duǒ	躲	V to hide (oneself), avoid (being seen by) 18
duōshì	多事	V meddlesome 12

E:

ér	而	CONJ whereas, but, on the other hand 14
érqiě	而且	MA moreover, and also 1
érxífu	儿媳妇/兒媳婦	N daughter-in-law 12

F:

fā	发/發	V to issue 18
fā dàshuǐ	发大水/發大水	VP to flood 13
fā//cái	发财/發財	VO to make a fortune; get rich 10
fàng	放	V to release; set off 10
fàng biānpào	放鞭炮	VP to set off firecrackers 10
fángdōng	房东/房東	N landlord (of a rented house or building) 7
fángkè	房客	N tenant 7
fāngmiàn	方面	N aspect, area 9
fāngshì	方式	N style (of doing something) 16
fàng//xīn	放心	VO/SV to rest assured, feel relieved 1
fángzū	房租	N rent (for a house or room) 7
fāpiào	发票/發票	N (sales) receipt 8
fā//shāo	发烧/發燒	VO to have a fever 4
fāxiàn	发现/發現	V/N to discover, find; discovery, finding 5
fāzhǎn	发展/發展	V/N to develop; development 9
fèi	费/費	N fee 7
fēi...bùkě	非...不可	IE must; insist on 12
fēijī	飞机/飛機	N airplane 1
fēnbié	分别	V/N/A to separate; separation; separately, respectively 1
fēngjǐng	风景/風景	N scenery, landscape 16
fēngsú	风俗/風俗	N custom, convention 10
fēnjī	分机/分機	N (of phone system) extension 6
fǒuzé	否则/否則	CONJ otherwise 17

fǔdǎo	辅导/輔導	V/N to tutor, guide; tutoring (giving guidance) 15
fù//kuǎn	付款	VO to make payment 17
fùxí	复习/複習	V/N to review (lessons); review 5
fùzá	复杂/複雜	ADJ complicated, complex 13
fùzé	负责/負責	V be responsible (for), in charge of 9

G:

gāisǐ	该死/該死	IE [colloq.] damn (lit. "deserve death") 6
gǎn	敢	AV to dare to 2
gānbābā	干巴巴/乾巴巴	ADJ dry and dull 5
gānjìng	干净/乾淨	SV be clean (洗干净,RV wash clean) 4
gǎnjué	感觉/感覺	V/N to feel, sense (that); feeling 18
gǎnkuài	赶快/趕快	A hurriedly, quickly 2
gǎnmào	感冒	N/V flu, cold; to have a cold/flu 4
gǎnqíng	感情	N emotion, feeling 5
gǎnxiè	感谢/感謝	V/N to thank, be grateful for; thank, appreciation 18
gàobié	告别	VO/N to bid farewell, say goodbye; farewell 1
gāodiǎn	糕点/糕點	N pastry 8
gāojí	高级/高級	ADJ high level/rank, advanced, advanced level 1
gāoyǎ	高雅	ADJ elegant 2
gè	各	PRON/A each 16
gēn	跟	V to follow 5
gēnběn	根本	A [not] at all 12
gèng bié shuō	更别说/更別說	A let alone, to say nothing of 12
gēqǔ	歌曲	N song 5
gōngkè	功课/功課	N course work, homework assignment 5
gōngsī	公司	N company 9
gōngxǐ	恭喜	IE "Congratulations!" (said on New Year's Day, birthdays, weddings, graduations, etc.) 10
gòngxiàn	贡献/貢獻	V/N to contribute; contribution (in abstract sense) 18
gōngyù	公寓	N apartment; apartment building 7
gōngyuán	公园/公園	N park 7
guà	挂/掛	V. hang; hang up (a phone); to ring off (sb. On the phone) 6
guǎi	拐	V to make a turn (in direction) 7
guàibude	怪不得	IE no wonder... (= 难怪/難怪) 4
guǎn	管	V to manage, take care [of a matter], in charge of 3

guàn	-惯/-慣	RVE be accustomed to / be in the habit of ...; (吃惯了,睡惯了) 5
Guǎngdōng	广东/廣東	PW (name of a province in China) 14
guǎnggào	广告/廣告	N advertisement 7
guǎn xiánshì	管闲事/管閒事	VP to butt into other people's business 3
guānyú	关于/關於	CONJ/CV regarding,about, concerning 17
gǔdài	古代	TW ancient times 13
guǐ	鬼	N ghosts 10
guì	贵/貴	BF [court.] your distinguished... 17
guīdìng	规定/規定	V/N to make it a rule that; rule, regulation 5
guìfāng	贵方/貴方	NP your side (the opposite party in a negotiation) 17
guìgōngsī	贵公司/貴公司	NP your distinguished company 17
guīju	规矩/規矩	N norms, etiquette, unwritten rules 11
gùkè	顾客/顧客	N customer, client 8
gǔlǎo	古老	ADJ ancient 10
gǔlì	鼓励/鼓勵	V/N to encourage; encouragement 18
guō	锅/鍋	N (Chinese) cooking pot, pan, "wok" 14
guò	过/過	V to observe (a holiday, birthday, etc.) 8
-guòletóu	-过了头/-過了頭	VP to overdo...; have overdone -睡过了头 oversleep 5
guójì	国际/國際	MOD international 17
guò//jié	过节/過節	VO to observe the holiday 8
guò//nián	过年/過年	VO to observe the New Year 10
guòqù	过去/過去	TW in the past, formerly 9
guǒrén	果仁	N nuts 8
gùyòng	雇(用)/僱(用)	V to hire (for employment) 9

H:

hāhā	哈哈	ON Ha, ha! 1
hái kěyǐ	还可以/還可以	IE so-so, passable 2
hǎo...	好...	A [for emphasis] so..., terribly, awfully 6
hǎogǎn	好感	N good impression or feelings (about a person) 12
hàomǎ	号码/號碼	N number (room, phone, etc.); code 6
hǎoxiào	好笑	ADJ be funny, amusing 1
hǎozài	好在	MA [colloq.] fortunately, luckily 5
hébì	何必	QW [rhetorical] What's the point...? (It's not necessary...) 12
hélǐ	合理	ADJ reasonable, fair 15
hépíng	和平	ADJ/N peaceful; peace 5
hézhuāng(de)	盒装(的)/盒裝(的)	box-packed; boxed 8

hézi	盒子	N box 8
hézuò	合作	V/N to co-operate; co-operation 17
hóngbāo	红包/紅包	N "red envelope" (used for giving money as a gift) 10
hóngshāo	红烧/紅燒	VP to stew with soysauce 14
hòu	厚/厚	ADJ (of flat objects) thick 12
hū	呼	V to exhale 4
hú	湖	N lake 16
huāhuā lùlù	花花绿绿/花花綠綠	PHR in bright, "loud" colors 16
huángdì	皇帝	N emperor 13
huángguā	黃瓜	N cucumber 14
huánjìng	环境/環境	N environment 4
huānsònghuì	欢送会/歡送會	N farewell party 18
huānyíng	欢迎 /歡迎	V/N to welcome; welcome 2
huàxué	化学/化學	N/ADJ chemistry; chemical 14
Huáyì	华裔/華裔	N citizen of Chinese origin 1
huàzhuāng	化装/化裝	V to disguise 15
huì	会/會	AV will/would, may/might, be likely 1
huì	会/會	N meeting, conference, party 8
huì	会/會	N party, conference; committee 15
hūn	荤/葷	N [lit] cooked food containing meat or fish 14
huòdān	货单/貨單	N inventory, order form ("list of merchandise") 17
huódòng	活动/活動	N activities, events 10
huòzhě	或者	CONJ or (as in either...or...) 4
hùzhào	护照/護照	N passport 1

J:

jí	-级/-級	BF level, rank 1
jí	急	V/SV to panic, worry; worried, anxious 14
jiàgé	价格/價格	N price 15
jiājù	家具/傢具	N furniture 7
jiājiào	家教	N private tutor 15
jiàn	建	V to build, establish 16
jiǎn	减/減	V to reduce, deduct, minus 8
jiǎnchá	检查/檢查	V/N to examine, inspect; checkup, inspection 4
jiǎnféi	减肥/減肥	VO to go on diet ("reduce fat") 8
jiāng	姜/薑	N ginger 14
jiàng	酱/醬	N thick sauce made from soybeans and flour etc. 14

jiàngdī	降低	V/RV to lower, bring down (price, standard, etc.) 17
jiǎng//huà	讲话/講話	VO/N to give speech, to talk; speech, talk 18
jiānglái	将来/將來	PW/N in the future; future 18
jiàngyóu	酱油/醬油	N soysauce 14
jiàn//miàn	见面/見面	VO to meet (someone), see 1
jiāo	交	V to submit, turn in; pay (rent, etc.) 7
jiǎo	角/角	N horn (of an animal) 13
jiǎo	角/角	N corner 15
jiāo péngyou	交朋友	VP to make friends 3
jiāoliú	交流	N exchange (of culture, thoughts, etc.) 18
jiǎozi	饺子/餃子	N (Chinese) dumpling 10
jiàqī	假期	N vacation (period) 16
jiāshàng	加上	MA/V plus the fact that; in addition; to add 5
jiātíng	家庭	N family 12
jiàzi	架子	N airs, haughty manner 11
jiàzi dà	架子大	IE put on airs; overbearing; insolent 11
jìde	记得/記得	V to remember 18
jīdòng	激动/激動	V/ADJ to get excited; excited 18
jiē	接	V to pick up/meet (sb. at a station, airport, etc.); to receive (mail, phone call, etc.) 2
jiē	接	V to connect; to answer (phone) 6
jié	节/節	BF holiday, festival 8
jiè	借/藉	V by means of, take (opportunity/ advantage to do sth.) 3
-jiè	-界	SUFF world, field, circle (自然界，报界) 13
jiéguǒ	结果/結果	MA/N consequently, as a result; result 4
jiéhūn	结婚/結婚	VO to get married, to marry 3
jiěkāi	解开/解開	V to untie, unfasten 4
jièkǒu	借口/藉口	N an excuse, a pretext 6
jiérì	节日/節日	N holiday, festival 10
jiéshù	结束/結束	V to end; (sth.) come to an end 18
jiēxiànyuán	接线员/接線員	N (phone) operator 6
jiēzhe	接着	MA subsequently, then, immediately, next 7
jìhuà	计划/計劃	V/N to plan; plan, plot 14
jīhuì	机会/機會	N chance, opportunity 3
jìjié	季节/季節	N season (shortened as 季 in 四季, 春季) 16
jìmò	寂寞	ADJ lonely 5
-jīn	-金	BF (lit. "gold") money, currency, a fund (used as N-Suf.) 7

jīngguò	经过/經過	CV by way of, via (can be shortened as 经) 16
jīngjì	经济/經濟	ADJ/N economical; economics, economy 3
jīnglǐ	经理/經理	N (business) manager (see notes) 9
jīngxǐ	惊喜/驚喜	N (delightful) surprise 17
jīngyàn	经验/經驗	N experience 9
jìngzhēng	竞争/競爭	V/N to compete; competition 17
jìnkǒu	进口/進口	V/N to import; import 9
jǐnkuài	尽快/儘快	A as soon as possible, soon 5
jìnrù	进入/進入	V to enter (syn. compound) 10
jìnxíng	进行/進行	V to proceed (to), carry on (with) 17
jǐnzhāng	紧张/緊張	ADJ nervous, tense 9
jìrán	既然	MA since (it is the case) 10
jìsuànjī	计算机/計算機	N computer (used in China) 15
jìxù	继续/繼續	V to continue (doing) 18
jì...yòu...	既...又 ...	A both... and ... 15
jízhōng	集中	V/N to concentrate; concentration 13
jù	据/據	CV according to, based on 13
jùhuì	聚会/聚會	V/N to get together; get-together, assembly, party 8
jù...suǒzhī	据...所知/據...所知	VP according to what sb. knows 13
jǔxíng	举行/舉行	V [formal] to hold (party, meeting, etc.) 15

K:

kāi	开/開	V to make out (a list, prescription, check) 4
kāibàn	开办/開辦	V to start or set up [a school, business, etc.] 15
kāi//huā	开花/開花	VO to blossom 16
kāixīn	开心/開心	ADJ happy, delighted 11
kànshàngqu	看上去	VP to look (young, tired, etc.) 7
kào	靠	V to lean against; to depend on 11
kàojìn	靠近	RV to get (physically) close to (sb. /sth.) 11
kǎoshang	考上	RV to pass (the entrance exam) 15
ké	咳	V cough 4
kě-	可-	BF -able, -ible 12
kě'ài	可爱/可愛	ADJ lovable, cute 12
kěkào	可靠	ADJ reliable 17
Kěkǒu Kělè	可口可乐/可口可樂	N (transliteration of) Coca Cola 8
késou	咳嗽	V/N to cough; cough 4
kètīng	客厅/客廳	N living-room, parlor 7

kèzhì	克制	V/N restrain, suppress; restraint, suppression 2
kǒnglóng	恐龙/恐龍	N dinosaur 13
kǒuyǔ	口语/口語	N spoken language 1
kòuzi	扣子	N (clothes) button 4
kū	哭	V to cry 18
Kūnmíng	昆明	PW (name of city in China) 16

L:

là	辣	ADJ (spicy) hot 14
láibují	来不及/來不及	RV [colloq.] cannot make it in time (to do sth.) 12
lán	栏/欄	BF (bulletin, newspaper) column, section 15
lè	乐/樂	V to have fun, amuse oneself 8
léi	雷	N thunder 13
lí	离/離	CV (distance) from (in space/time) 2
lǐ	礼/禮	N rite, etiquette 11
lì	历/曆	calendar (used as N-Suf.) 10
liàn'ài	恋爱/戀愛	V/N be in love; romantic love 3
lián	连/連	CV including, with......included 4
liáng	量	V to measure (temperature, length, etc.) 4
liàng	量	N quantity, volume 17
liángbàn	凉拌/涼拌	VP to make a cold dish by mixing vegetable and sauce 14
liángkuài	凉快/涼快	ADJ cool and comfortable (in summer and fall) 16
liángxìng	凉性/涼性	N "cool-natured" (of food or Chinese medicine) 14
liánluò	联络/聯絡	V/N to get in touch; contact (between people) 9
liáotiān	聊天	VO to chat 5
liǎojiě	了解	V to know well; to learn about 11
Lǐ Dàwéi	李大为/李大爲	N (Chinese name of) David Leigh 1
lǐ duō rén bú guài	礼多人不怪/禮多人不怪	PH "You can't be too polite" (lit. "People don't blame you for being too polite") 11
lìhai	厉害/厲害	ADJ severe 4
lǐmào	礼貌/禮貌	N (good) manners, courtesy 11
lǐngdǎo	领导/領導	V/N to lead; leader; leadership 18
línghuó	灵活/靈活	ADJ flexible, agile 15
Lín Hóng	林红/林紅	N (name of a person) 2
lìngwài	另外	MA in addition, besides 4
lìngwài	另(外)	ADJ another, the other... 13

lìqi	力气/力氣	N. physical strength 4
liú	留	V to leave (sth. for sb.)
Liú Dōng	刘东/劉東	N (name of a person) 10
liú// huà	留话/留話	VP to leave a (verbal) message 6
liúlì	流利	ADJ fluent 9
liúxíng	流行	ADJ popular (song, fashion, etc.) 5
liú//xué	留学/留學	VO to study abroad 1
lóng	龙/龍	N dragon 13
lù	鹿	N deer (M. zhī 只) 13
lǚlìbiǎo	履历表/履歷表	N resume, curriculum vitae 9
luōsuo	啰嗦/囉嗦	ADJ [of a person] repetitious and fussy 7
lùyīnjī	录音机/錄音機	N tape recorder (录音,V/N to make a tape recording; recording, tape) 5
lǚyóu	旅游/旅遊	V/N to travel (for pleasure); tour/travel, 16

M:

ma	嘛	p (Particle suggesting obviousness) 4
máfan	麻烦/麻煩	V/N/SV to trouble; (put sb. to some) trouble; annoyance; troublesome 6
Mǎlì	玛丽/瑪麗	N (transliteration of) Mary, Marie 8
mǎlù	马路/馬路	N boulevard, avenue 7
mán	蛮/蠻	A [colloq.] quite, rather, pretty (good,etc.) 12
mǎn	满/滿	ADJ be full 16
mǎnyì	满意/滿意	ADJ satisfied, content, happy with 7
màoyì	贸易/貿易	N (large scale) trade 17
měilì	美丽/美麗	ADJ/N beautiful; beauty 16
méi xiǎng dào	没想到	IE surprisingly, to sb.'s surprise; unexpectedly 18
mén dāng hù duì	门当户对/門當戶對	PH a perfect match in social status (for marriage) 12
miàn	面	N side 2
miàn	面/麵	N noodles; flour, dough 4
miànshì	面试/面試	V/N to have a (job) interview; (job) interview 9
miàntán	面谈/面談	V/N to talk face-to-face; face-to-face talk 9
míngmíng	明明	A clearly, obviously 2
mínzú	民族	N ethnicity(shortened as族 after a name) 16
mìshū	秘书/秘書	N secretary 9
míxìn	迷信/迷信	ADJ/N superstitious; superstition 10

N:

nǎiyóu	奶油	N butter, cream 8

Nánjīng	南京	PW (name of city in China)
nánshòu	难受/難受	ADJ sad, unbearable, intolerable 4
nèiháng	内行	N/ expert; skilled (ant.外行 amateurish) 14
nénggàn	能干/能幹	ADJ capable, able 3
nénglì	能力	N ability, capability (abbr. As力 in compounds) 9
niàn	念/唸	V to read aloud, chant (poem, etc.) 5
niánlíng	年龄/年齡	N age (of a person) 15
niǎo	鸟/鳥	N bird (M. zhī 只) 13
nuǎnhuo	暖和	ADJ (temperature) warm (in winter and spring) 16
nǔlì	努力	V to strive, work hard (to achieve sth.) 5

P:

pá	爬	V to climb, crawl 16
páizi	牌	N sign; brand (of a product) 2
pànwàng	盼望	V/N to look forward to; expectation 6
pǎo	跑	V/RVE run, run away; (run) away 10
pèi	配	V to match 12
pèijiàn	配件	N parts, component (of a machine) 17
pí	皮	N skin; leather 4
piàn	片	M piece, slice,etc. 16
piānpiān	偏偏	MA 4
piāo	漂	V to drift, float (on water)
piào	票	N ticket 1
píjiǔ	啤酒	N beer 8
-pǐn	-品	BF -stuff, item (Noun-Suffix) 8
píng	瓶	M/N bottle, jar 12
píngcháng	平常	ADJ/MA normal, usual, ordinary; normally, usually 14
pútao	葡萄	N grapes 8

Q:

qī	期	M (school,course, etc.) term 15
qì	气/氣	N air, gas, vapor 4
qiáng	强/強	ADJ strong, powerful 9
qiānwàn	千万/千萬	A [colloq.] (Do/Don't...) by all/any means 11
qiānzhèng	签证/簽證	N visa 1
qiǎokelì	巧克力	N (transliteration of) chocolate 8
qiàtán	洽谈/洽談	V/N[formal] to negotiate (business); negotiation 17

qícì	其次	MA secondly 18
qiē	切	V to cut, slice 14
qìhòu	气候/氣候	N climate 16
qījiān	期间/期間	TW during [a period of time] 10
Qīngdǎo	青岛/青島	N (name of a Chinese city in Shandong, famous for its beer) 8
qǐngjià	请假/請假	VO to ask for a leave of absence 4
qíngkuàng	情况/情況	N situation, condition, status 3
qīngsōng	轻松/輕鬆	ADJ light-hearted, relaxed, easy 8
qìngzhù	庆祝/慶祝	V/N to celebrate; celebration 10
qīnqi	亲戚/親戚	N relatives (of extended family) 1
qīnwěn	亲吻/親吻	V/N to kiss; kiss (colloq.: 亲) 11
qíshí	其实/其實	MA actually, as a matter of fact 6
qǐshì	启事/啓事	N a notice, written announcement (to public) 15
qìshuǐ	汽水	N soda (carbonated beverage) 8
qítā	其他	SP other (people, things, places, etc.) 11
qízhōng	其中	PW among them; in which 2
quánlì	权力/權力	N (authority) power 13
què	却	A but, however (used withetc.) 14

R:

ràng//bù	让步/讓步	VO to yield, compromise 17
rènao	热闹/熱鬧	ADJ (atmosphere) festive, lively, noisy 8
rénjiā	人家	N [colloq.] the other person, other people; a 3rd person or the speaker himself/herself) 6
rènwéi	认为/認爲	EV to think that..., believe that... 5
rèqíng	热情/熱情	ADJ warm-hearted, friendly 5
rìqī	日期	N date 2
rìzi	日子	N (special) day(birthday, anniversary, etc.) 8
rú	如	EV such as 10
rù	入	V [lit.] to enter (syn. of 进) 10

S:

shǎ	傻	ADJ silly, foolish 1
shǎn	闪/閃	V to sparkle, flash 16
shǎn//diàn	闪电/閃電	V/N to have lightning; lightning 13
shàng//bān	上班	VO to go to work, to work (in one's office) 9
shāngdiàn	商店	N store 7

shàng//huǒ	上火	VO [Chin. med.] to suffer from too much internal heat (with symptoms such as constipation, or inflammation of the nasal and oral cavities) 14
shāngliang	商量	V to talk over (for a solution) 7
shàngmiàn	上面	PW on top of, on, above (syn. 上头,上边); 2
shāngyè	商业/商業	N business, commerce 9
shāng xīn	伤心/傷心	VO/ADJ to hurt feelings; sad, heartbroken 6
shǎo	少	V to lack, be short of 1
shāoděng	稍等	PH "One moment,please" "I'll be with you shortly", "Hold on" 6
shǎoshù	少数/少數	N the minority 16
shāowēi	稍微	A slightly (can be shortened as稍) 9
shěbude	舍不得/捨不得	RV to hate to part with, reluctant to let go 18
shèjiāo	社交	V/N to socialize; socializing 11
shēn	深	ADJ deep 13
shēn	参/參	N ginseng 14
shěng	省	N province 16
shēng//bìng	生病	VO to fall ill, get sick 4
shěnghuì	省会/省會	N capital of a province (首都is used for a country) 16
shēngyin	声音/聲音	N sound, voice, noise 10
shēnqǐng	申请/申請	V/N to apply (for); application 1
shí	时/時	TW o'clock (formal use of 点钟) 8
shǐ	使	V to make (sb/sth.)..., cause (sb. to VP) (syn. of 让) 7
-shì	-式	BF –style 7
shìchǎng	市场/市場	N market 9
shìfǒu	是否	QW whether or not (lit. form of是不是) 17
Shílín	石林	PW Stone Forest (name of a scenic place) 16
shípǐn	食品	N food 8
shí quán shí měi	十全十美	PH (of a person or thing) perfect, good in every aspect 12
shítáng	食堂	N cafeteria (of a school, hospital, etc.) 5
shítou	石头/石頭	N stone, rock 16
shìyè	事业/事業	N career, a pursuit 12
shìyèxīn	事业心/事業心	N ambition, devotion to one's pursuit 12
shìyìng	适应/適應	V/ADJ to get adjusted to; accustomed to 4
shòu	受	V/CV to receive; by (see Structural Focus) 8
shòubuliǎo	受不了	RV can't tolerate or stand 12
shōudào	收到	RV to receive [mail, gift, etc.] 5
shòuhuòyuán	售货员/售貨員	N store clerk, salesperson 8

shōushi	收拾	V to put (things) in order, tidy up 1
shóu/shú	熟	ADJ ripe, [food] cooked; familiar 11
shóuxi/shúxi	熟悉	V/ADJ to be/become quite familiar (with), know sth. or sb. well; acquainted with 3
shǒuxiān	首先	MA first of all, firstly 18
shǔ	数/數	V to count (numbers etc.) 6
shūdāizi	书呆子/書呆子	N bookworm, nerd (lit. "book idiot") 12
shuǐdiànfèi	水电费/水電費	N utility cost ("water and electricity fee") 7
shuǐtǔ bù fú	水土不服	PH negative physical reactions caused by a new environment ("The water and soil don't agree with you.") 4
shuōbudìng	说不定/說不定	MA maybe, perhaps 3
shuōmíng	说明/說明	V to indicate 11
shùnlì	顺利/順利	ADJ/A (progress of a matter) smooth; smoothly, without a hitch 5
shūxiě	书写/書寫	N [formal] writing (skill) 9
shùyǔ	术语/術語	N professional terminology, jargon 9
sījī	司机/司機	N chauffeur, driver 2
sūnzi	孙子/孫子	N grandchild 12
Sìchuān	四川	PW (name of a province in China) 14
sù	素	N [lit] vegetarian food, vegetable food 14
suān	酸	ADJ sour 14
suàn	算	V to count; to be considered as 4
suàn	蒜	N garlic 14
suànfǎ	算法	N calculation, way of calculating 10
suànle	算了	IE "Forget it." "Never mind." 6
suíbiàn	随便/隨便	ADJ/A casual, informal; do as one pleases; randomly, casually, carelessly 3
suí nǐ biàn	随你便/隨你便	PH do whatever you like, do as you please 14
sùshè	宿舍	N dormitory, dorm-room 5

T:

tā	它	N it (used for animals etc.) 13
tàidu	态度/態度	N attitude 5
Táiwān	台湾/台灣	PW Taiwan 3
tándelái	谈得来/談得來	RV [colloq.] share common interest 12
tán liàn'ài	谈恋爱/談戀愛	VO to get romantically involved, to date 3
táng	糖	N sugar; candy 14
tàng	烫/燙	ADJ be scalding hot, hotter than normal 4
tào	套	M set of (furniture, books, etc.); suit (of clothing, etc.) 7

tǎolùn	讨论/討論	V/N to discuss (issues); discussion 13
tèdiǎn	特点/特點	N characteristics 13
téng	疼	V (a body part) to ache, hurt, pain 4
tèsè	特色	N special (attractive) features 16
tián	甜	ADJ sweet 8
tiáojiàn	条件/條件	N condition, term 4
tiào//wǔ	跳舞	VO to dance 8
tígōng	提供	V supply, provide 15
tímù	题目/題目	N title, topic 13
tīng	厅/廳	N hall, parlor 7
tíng	停	V to stop 5
tīng qǐlái	听起来/聽起來	VP to sound [like...] 11
tǐtiē	体贴/體貼	V be considerate (of others' needs, feelings) 12
tǐwēn	体温/體溫	N body temperature 4
tōng	通	V get through (on telephone) 6
tōng qíng dá lǐ	通情达理/通情達理	PH (of a person) understanding and reasonable 12
tóngshì	同事	V/N to work at the same place/co-worker, colleague 17
tóngwū	同屋	N room-mate (in Taiwan: 室友) 5
tóngxué	同学/同學	N classmate, fellow student (同, "same" prefixed to nouns) 2
tǒngyī	统一/統一	V/N to unify; uniformity,unification; unity 13
tóngyì	同意	V to agree (with) 13
tōngzhī	通知	V/N to notify; notification, notice (to specific group or person) 15
tù	吐	V to vomit, throw up 4
tǔ	吐	V to spit, spit something out 4
tuántuán zhuàn	团团转/團團轉	ADJ (so busy that you) run around in circles 1
tuánjù	团聚/團聚	V to get together, reunite 8
tuījiàn	推荐/推薦	V/N to recommend; recommendation 8
tuīxiāo	推销/推銷	V to (promote and) sell, to market 9
tūrán	突然	MA/ADJ suddenly, abruptly; abrupt 2

W:

wǎng	往	CV toward, to, in the direction of 7
wángguó	王国/王國	N kingdom 16
wàng zǐ chéng lóng	望子成龙/望子成龍	PH to hope one's child will amount to something 13
wǎnhuì	晚会/晚會	N evening party 8
wànwàn	万万/萬萬	A by all/any means, under any circumstances 12
wèi	胃	N stomach 14

wéi/wèi	喂	INTERJ Hello! (mostly used on the phone) 6
wèidao	味道	N flavor 14
wèi...(ér)...	为...(而)/爲...(而)	CV-A. for (the sake/purpose of...) [therefore]... 3
wèishēng	卫生/衛生	SV/N sanitary; sanitation; hygienic, hygiene 4
wèiyú	位于/位於	V [formal] be located at 16
wén	闻/聞	V to smell 14
wēnhé	温和	ADJ mild 14
wènhòu	问候/問候	V to ask after someone 10
wénmíng	闻名/聞名	ADJ be well-known 16
wēnróu	温柔	ADJ (person) gentle, tender 15
wú	无/無	A [lit] no, without (=没有) 13
wù	-物	BF object, thing (used as N-Suf.) 13
wú chù bú zài	无处不在/無處不在	PH ubiquitous 13
Wú Hǎilín	吴海琳/吳海琳	N (Chinese name of) Helen Wu 1

X:

xǐ	洗	V to wash 4
xī	吸	V inhale 4
xì	系	N department (in a college) 8
Xī'ān	西安	PW (name of city in China) 16
Xiàcháo	夏朝	N Xia Dynasty (ca. 21-16 century B.C.) 13
xiàng	向	CV toward, to 2
xiàng	项/項	M item (Measure Word for goods, topics, etc.) 17
xiàng(zi)	巷(子)	N alley, narrow street 7
xiàngzhēng	象征/象徵	V/N to symbolize; symbol; symbolism 13
xiànxiàng	现象/現象	N phenomenon, sign 13
xiàtiān	夏天	N summer 16
xià//xuě	下雪	VO to snow 16
xián	咸/鹹	ADJ salty 8
xiāng	香	N/ADJ aroma,smell of cooked food; aromatic 14
xiǎng	响/響	V/ADJ (sth.) to make a sound; loud 10
xiāngchǔ	相处/相處	V to be together [w/sb.] for a period of time 17
xiǎngniàn	想念	V [formal] to miss, long for 8
xiāngsì	相似	ADJ similar 13
xiāngxìn	相信	V to believe 2
xiǎngxiàng	想象	V/N to imagine; imagination 12

xiāo	削	V to scrape, peel, pare 4
xiǎoshí	小时/小時	N. hour (syn. of 钟头) 6
xiāoxi	消息	N news (as in "good news") 15
xiǎoxīn	小心	SV be careful 14
xiè dù(zi)	泻肚(子)/瀉肚(子)	VO [colloq.] to have diarrhea (肚子, stomach, belly) 4
xīfāng	西方	PW the West (re. western hemisphere) 13
xíguàn	习惯/習慣	V/N to get used to; habit 1
-xīn	-心	SUF -minded, [have] a conscience of 15
xìnfēng	信封	N envelope 5
-xíng	-型	BF -size; -type (used as N. suf.) 16
-xìng	-性	BF -natured, -ness, gender (used as N-Suf.) 14
xīngfèn	兴奋/興奮	ADJ/N excited, thrilled; excitement 1
xìngqíng	性情	N disposition 5
xìngqù	兴趣/興趣	N interest (in sth.) 9
xíngxiàng	形象	N image 13
xīnkǔ	辛苦	ADJ/N laborious, toilsome; toil 2
xīnshì	心事	N something weighing on one's mind 12
xīnshuǐ	薪水	N salary 9
xīnxiān	新鲜	SV fresh 4
xīnxiě/xīnxuè	心血	N effort, hardwork ("mind and blood") 18
xìnxīn	信心	N confidence, faith 9
xīyān	吸烟/吸煙	VO to smoke (cigarette or cigar) 7
xīyǐn	吸引	V to attract, be appealing to 16
xuélì	学历/學歷	N educational background 8
xuéqī	学期/學期	N semester, term, duration (of a course, etc.) 15
xuéwèn	学问/學問	N knowledge, learning 12
xuézhě	学者/學者	N scholar 13
xùnliàn	训练/訓練	V/N to train; training 9
xūyào	需要	V/N to need; needs 9

Y:

yà	亚/亞	Asia (used as suffix, but also as prefix (亚洲, Yàzhōu, Asia) 3
Yàkě	亚可/亞可	N (one common trans-literation for 'Jacques') 2
Yǎkè	雅克	N (another common trans-literation for 'Jacques') 2
yán	盐/鹽	N salt 14
Yáng	杨/楊	N (a Chinese surname) 7
yángé	严格/嚴格	ADJ strict, harsh (can be shortened to 严) 5
yángguāng	阳光/陽光	N sunlight 16

yánglì	阳历/陽曆	N solar calendar 10
yàngzi	样子/樣子	N appearance, look 1
yǎnjìng	眼镜/眼鏡	N eye-glasses 12
yǎnjìngpiàn	眼镜片/眼鏡片	N. eye-glass lens 12
yánjiūsuǒ	研究所	N graduate/school institute (also 研究院) 12
yàofāng	药方/藥方	N prescription 4
yàojǐn	要紧/要緊	ADJ urgent, important 5
yāoqǐng	邀请/邀請	V/N to invite; invitation 8
yě jiùshì shuō	也就是说/也就是說	PH that is to say, that means, in other words 14
yèwù	业务/業務	N business activities, field stuff 9
yèzi	叶子/葉子	N leaf (of a tree) (shortened as 叶 after a name) 16
yī	医/醫	V to treat (a patient, an ailment);BF medical 4
yì	-裔	BF of descent 1
yìbān	一般	ADJ general, average, run of the mill 6
yǐjí	以及	CONJ and also, as well as 18
yílù shùnfēng	一路顺风/一路順風	PH "Bon voyage!" "Have a nice trip!" 1
yímín	移民	V/N to immigrate/emigrate; immigrant/emigrant 1
...yǐ nán	...以南	PW to the south of... 16
yīng	鹰/鷹	N eagle (M. zhī 只) 13
yíngyǎng	营养/營養	N nutrition, nourishment 14
yínháng	银行/銀行	N bank 7
yìngyāo	应邀/應邀	CV-O upon invitation ("respond to an invitation") 11
yīnlì	阴历/陰曆	lunar calendar 10
yǐnliào	饮料/飲料	N beverage 8
yǐnshí	饮食/飲食	N diet 14
yìnxiàng	印象	N impression (on one's mind) 13
yíqiè	一切	N all; everything 5
yīshēng	医生/醫生	N (medical) doctor, physician 4
yìshēng(zhōng)	一生(中)	N a life-time; all/throughout one's life 3
yìwài	意外	ADJ/N unexpected, accidental; accident 17
yīwùshì	医务室/醫務室	N clinic, medical office (of a school, company) 4
yìxìng	异性/異性	N the opposite sex 11
yōngbào	拥抱/擁抱	V to hold in arms, hug, embrace 11
yóu	油	ADJ/N oily, greasy; oil, grease 8
yóu	游	V to swim 13
yóu	由	CV from (lit. form of 从) 16
yǒu dàolǐ	有道理	VP/ADJ (sth.) to make sense, be logical 13

yóujú	邮局/郵局	N post office 7
yóukè	游客/遊客	N tourist, traveler 16
yǒuqù	有趣/有趣	ADJ interesting, amusing 12
yǒuyì	有意	V/ADJ have interest; interested 15
yóuyú	由于/由於	CONJ due to, because (of) 13
yǔ	-语/-語	BF language, speech (used as N-suf) 1
-yú	-于/-於	V-SUF [lit] than (as in 低于) 17
yuǎn	远/遠	ADJ far 2
yuángù	缘故/緣故	N reason, cause 13
yuánlái	原来/原來	MA as it turned out, "so that's the reason for ..." 11
yuánlái	原来/原來	ADJ/MA original, initial; originally, initially 12
yuánliàng	原谅/原諒	V to forgive 18
yuányīn	原因	N reason, cause 3
yuǎnyuǎnde	远远地/遠遠地	A (do...) from a distance 16
yuē	约/約	V to make an appointment 1
yuèdú	阅读/閱讀	V/N. to read; reading 9
yuēhǎo	约好/約好	RV to fix time/place, etc. for a meeting 1
yuèliang	月亮	N the moon 8
yuè xīn	月薪	N monthly salary 9
yúkuài	愉快	ADJ/A happy; happily 16
Yúnnán shěng	云南省/雲南省	PW (name of province in China) 16
yúshì	于是/於是	CONJ so, then, thereupon, therefore 9
yùshì	浴室	N bathroom (with or without toilet) 7

Z:

zàishuō	再说/再說	MA furthermore, besides 12
zāole	糟了	IE "Oh, darn it!" 14
zēngzhǎng	增长/增長	V to grow, increase 16
zěnmebàn	怎么办/怎麼辦	PH "What to do?" 14
zérèn	责任/責任	N responsibility, duty 15
zhá	炸	V to deep-fry 14
zhǎngbèi	长辈/長輩	N elders ("the senior generation"), seniors 10
zhàngfu	丈夫	N husband 12
zhāng zuǐ	张嘴/張嘴	VO to open the mouth 4
zhàn xiàn	占线/佔線	VO [of phone line] be busy, occupied 6
Zhào	赵/趙	N (Chinese surname) 12

zhào	照	V to shine, illuminate 16
Zhào Déshēng	赵德生/趙德生	N (name of a person) 12
zhàogù	照顾/照顧	V/N to look after; care for; attend to 12
zhāojí	着急	V/ADJ to worry; be worried 6
zháo// liáng	着凉/着涼	VO to catch cold 4
zhǎo//qián	找钱/找錢	VO to give change 8
zhāo//shēng	招生	VO to enroll new students 15
zhékòu	折扣	N discount 17
zhēng	征/徵	V [formal] to solicit publicly, to seek 15
zhèngfǔ	政府	N government 16
zhènghǎo	正好	A/MA just at the right time; just right; coincidentally, it just so happens that 3
zhèngmíng	证明/證明	V/N to prove, certify; certifying letter 4
zhěngqí	整齐/整齊	SV neat, orderly 7
zhèngshū	证书/證書	N certificate 18
zhēn yàomìng	真要命	IE It's awful! It drives me crazy! 4
zhìliàng	质量/質量	N quality 17
zhínü	侄女	N niece 12
zhīshi	知识/知識	N knowledge, learning 16
zhíwù	职务/職務	N (job) position 9
zhǐyào	只要	MA as long as (often used with 就) 7
zhǒng	种/種	M type, kind 1
Zhōngqiūjié	中秋节/中秋節	N The Moon Festival (lit. "mid-autumn fes tival" (15th day of the 8th lunar month)) 8
zhōngshì	中式	MOD Chinese-styled (e.g.,中式家具) 7
zhòngshì	重视/重視	V to regard as important, take sth. Seriously 5
zhōngxīn	中心	N center 2
zhù	祝	V to wish (as in "I wish you luck") 1
zhǔ	煮	V to boil, cook in water 14
zhuǎ/zhǎo	爪	N claw, paw 13
zhuǎn	转/轉	V to foward, transfer; (envelope) care fo (c/o) 5
zhuāngshì	装饰/裝飾	to decorate; decoration 10
zhùlǐ	助理	N assistant 9
zhǔnbèi	准备/準備	V/N to prepare; preparation 1
zhǔnshí	准时/準時	ADJ/A on time, punctual; punctually 11
zhǔxiū	主修	V/N to major (in); major (in college) 3

zhǔyào	主要	MOD/A main, major, essential; mainly, essentially 9
zhúyì	主意	N [colloq] idea 6
zhùyì	注意	V to pay attention to, watch 4
zǐ	紫	ADJ purple 16
zìcóng	自从/自從	MA (ever) since 6
zìdiǎn	字典	N dictionary 9
zìláishuǐ	自来水/自來水	N tap water 4
zīliào	资料/資料	N data, written information 17
zǐnǚ	子女	N [generic] children ("sons and daughters") 15
zìrán	自然	ADJ/A natural; naturally 1
zǐsūn	子孙/子孫	N offspring 13
zì yǐ wéi shì	自以为是/自以爲是	PH to regard oneself as right; disregard the opinions of others 3
zǒngsuàn	总算/總算	MA at long last, finally (for 总) 2
zǒngzhī	总之/總之	PH "to sum up", "in conclusion" 18
zū	租	V to rent 7
zuì	醉	V to get drunk; drunk 8
zūnjìng	尊敬	V/N to respect (person); respect (to a person) 11
zuò	做	V to be (a teacher, manager, mother , etc.) 9
zuò//kè	做客	VO to visit as an invited guest 11
zuóliào	作料	N side-ingredient, dressing (for cooking), seasoning 14
zuò//mèng	做梦/做夢	VO to dream 17